CONTROLLING YOUR DIVORCE

A book for the self-represented family law litigant

Knowledge is power.

Don't just get through your divorce. Control your divorce from beginning to end.

Table of Contents

Contents

Knowledge is power. 1
DISCLAIMERS: 6
ABOUT ME 7
WORDING IN BOOK 8
INTRODUCTION 9
   WHO THIS BOOK IS INTENDED FOR 10
   WHAT THIS BOOK IS INTENDED FOR 10
   HOW TO USE THIS BOOK 10
CHAPTER 1 - BEFORE DIVORCE 11
   Planning Your Divorce Before Anyone Files 11
   Custody/Legal Decision-Making/Parenting Time 13
   Financial Issues 21
CHAPTER 2 - PROCEDURES – RULES – STATUTES 30
   STATUTES 30
   Rules of Procedures 32
   Are You Legally Married? 33
   You Are Not Married, But You Have a Child Together 34
   Property Acquired Before Marriage 34
CHAPTER 3 - BEGINNING THE PROCESS 35
   Separating/Moving out 35
   Hiring Someone to Help with the Divorce 35
   Preparing Documents 37
   Changing the Judge 38
   Setting Up Your Case 38
   Involving Children 41

Trying To Negotiate a Settlement Before Filing or Immediately Thereafter. 42

CHAPTER 4 – ORDERS OF PROTECTION / RESTRAININGORDER / INJUNCTIONS 43

   Purpose of Order 43

   Sworn Testimony/Ex-Parte Hearing to Receive Order 44

   Contested Hearing Before Order 44

   Contested Hearing After Order 44

   Upheld Order 45

   Effect of Order on Family Case 45

   Quashed Order 45

   Expiration of Order 45

CHAPTER 5 - LEGAL DECISION-MAKING AND PARENTINGTIME 46

   Legal Decision-Making 46

   Parenting Time 46

   Custody Evaluations 47

   Best Interest Attorney / Guardian Ad Litem / Child's Attorney 48

   Drug and Alcohol Use and Abuse 49

   Parenting Plan 52

   Long-Distance Parenting Plan 73

CHAPTER 6 – CHILD SUPPORT 77

   Determining Child Support 77

   Tax Exemptions/Deductions/Credits 81

   Age of Majority 81

CHAPTER 7 – SPOUSAL MAINTENANCE/ALIMONY 84

   Vocational Evaluation 86

CHAPTER 8 - DIVISION OF ASSETS AND DEBTS 87

   Division of Assets 87

   Community Property or Jointly Owned Business 91

   Debt 93

CHAPTER 9 - MISCELLANEOUS ISSUES 95
Grandparent/Third Party Rights 95
Marital Waste 95
Attorney Fees and Costs 96

CHAPTER 10 - BUILDING A CASE 99
Discovery 99
Protective Order 119
How to use your discovery. 120
Disclosure 120

CHAPTER 11 – SETTLING OUTSIDE OF COURT 125
Mediation 125
Settlement Conference 130
Alternative Dispute Resolution (ADR) 130
Arbitration 131
Private Judge 131
Meet and Confer 132
Settlement Offers Between Parties 132

CHAPTER 12 – PREPARING FOR COURT 134
Trial Preparation 134
Evidence 139
Pre-Trial 142

CHAPTER 13 – TRIAL 147
Trial Procedure 147
Petitioner's case 150
Respondent's Case 156
Cross Examination 156
Evidence 158
Closing Arguments 163
Objections 163

CHAPTER 14 – FINAL ORDER OF THE COURT 167

CHAPTER 15 – APPEALS AND POST ORDER REMEDIES 168
   Setting aside the order;.. *168*
   Clarifying the order or Correcting an order *168*
   Reconsidering the order *169*
   Motion for New Trial *169*
   Appealing the order... *169*
CHAPTER 16 – FOLLOWING COURT ORDERS 171
CHAPTER 17 – POST DECREE PLEADINGS 172
   Modification of Legal Decision-Making or Parenting Time *172*
   Modification of Parenting Plan *173*
   Modification of Child Support... *173*
   Modification of Spousal Maintenance *174*
   Modification of the Divorce Decree *174*
CHAPTER 18 – MY TWO CENTS... 175

DISCLAIMERS:

- This book is not intended to give legal advice but to provide you with practical information when going through your divorce.
- Reading this book does not create an attorney client relationship.
- Please be sure to speak with an attorney in your area.
- I am licensed to practice law only in the state of Arizona.
- Although I may reference other states, my only experience is with Arizona Courts. But much of what is written in this book is applicable in all states. Just be sure to check your state's rules, procedures and statutes.
- I say check your local rules, or the rules in your jurisdiction, over and over in this book. The book is meant to be a roadmap to help guide you to the laws in your area. For instance, I will provide you with some ideas of what to do after an you receive an order that seems to be wrong. I won't tell you how to do it or the rules of your court, simply that there may be options for you to look at.
- Remember, laws change daily. Any laws or definitions listed in this book could change the next day. The purpose of the book is not to provide or explain the laws, but only to help guide you through the process.
- The laws that are listed should be verified by each reader at the time of reading or proceeding with a divorce/separation.
- Should you have any questions, you should seek input from an attorney in your area.

ABOUT ME

I have been practicing almost exclusively in Family Law since 2000. In 2018 I decided to focus my practice on preparing other attorneys' clients for hearings, depositions, custody evaluation, vocational evaluations and the like. Parents spend thousands of dollars on custody evaluations trying to obtain sole legal decision-making and the majority of parenting time, yet they are often ill prepared for the evaluations, and their participation in the evaluations while being unprepared sometimes do more harm than good to their case. If you are requesting custody/legal decision-making, make sure to get my book, Custody Evaluation Preparation, 2nd Edition. It will help you to present your best self to the evaluator and the court.

After writing the custody evaluation prep book, I realized that I could help self-represented litigants prepare for their divorce case just as I helped prepare parties for custody evaluations.

My objective is not to provide legal advice, but to help you present your best self and your best case if you choose to represent yourself in your divorce. This book should be used as a roadmap for you to help you find relevant laws and rules in your state.

WORDING IN BOOK

Although family law cases may include people who have never been married (referred to as "paternity" cases, for ease of reading and writing, I will use the word *divorce* to describe the separation and conflict which has given rise to the need to prepare yourself for litigation.

Further, although parents may be mother/father, dad/mom, partners, mother/mother, mom/mom or father/father, dad/dad, for ease of reading, and more so ease of writing, I will use mother/mom and/or father/dad and it should be understood to apply to all those relationships.

I will also be using words such as he/she and him/her interchangeably. This is only done for ease of writing and reading.

I will often be using the phrase "custody evaluation" for all types of evaluations that involve parenting, except where I speak specifically about different evaluations.

Finally, because Arizona and many other states have changed the terminology involved in family cases, such as "custody" to "legal decision-making" and "visitation" to "parenting time" when I speak of "legal decision-making" that term should be understood as including "custody"; and when I use the words "parenting time" that should be understood to include "visitation" and vice-versa.

The word "jurisdiction" refers to the location in which your divorce proceedings are or will be litigated.

INTRODUCTION

We have all heard statistics about the percentage of married people getting divorced. It seems as if 50% was the number for a long time. However, there is really no way to find a real accurate accounting because some states do not participate, so there is no "national divorce rate" that accounts for divorces in all states. The Center for Disease Control is the official government agency charged with tracking marriage and divorce statistics. Unfortunately, their statistics for both marriages and divorces is woefully lacking and do not include all the states. In fact, the CDC has provided statistics for the years 2000 - 2016 and in each year at least four states are not included. (https://www.cdc.gov/nchs/data/dvs/national_marriage_divorce_rates_00-16.pdf) California's numbers were never included and California has the largest population in the country[1].

Most of the divorces that take place in this country are completed without attorneys. Finding your way through a divorce without an attorney can be quite daunting. On the other hand, playing an attorney $200-$600 per hour (depending on where you are located) can be too expensive for most people. Some states permit document preparers and legal paraprofessionals to help which can provide for a less expensive alternative.

Although most jurisdictions have some type of self-help service, either online or at the Court, the services may not provide you with in depth information. In fact, most just provide the basics. However, if your soon to be ex is hiding money from you or refuses to provide you with documents, this book will help you figure out how to work through those issues.

It is important to remember that all jurisdictions have different laws and different procedures. This book is not a substitute for your responsibility to know those rules and laws. Instead, this book will help guide you and help you to learn how to find the rules in your jurisdiction and help you use those rules to your advantage.

From the very beginning, before you even file, you need to plan plan plan. This book will help you plan, organize and work your way through the divorce.

---

[1] http://worldpopulationreview.com/states/

WHO THIS BOOK IS INTENDED FOR

This book is intended for any person who is thinking about getting a divorce.

This book is intended for any person currently going through a divorce.

And, this book is for any person who is involved in post-decree litigation.

WHAT THIS BOOK IS INTENDED FOR

This book will help walk you through the process from the time you think about divorce, during the entire divorce, the appeal and even post decree filings. Although I am licensed in Arizona, the basic structure of the divorce process will be the same and I will provide you with practical tips to help you research and to help you prepare for hearings, evaluations, depositions and the like.

HOW TO USE THIS BOOK

This book is intended to be a roadmap to help you find rules and laws in your area. I will recommend over and over that you look at the rules in your jurisdiction or that you speak with a lawyer. I recommend that because I cannot possibly know all the laws, rules and procedures in all jurisdictions. However, that does not mean this book can't help you. There are many areas of litigation that have similar rules; such as rules on discovery, disclosure, expert witnesses, trial procedures and the like.

You can either read right through this book and mark pages that you might find important, or you can look at this book's table of contents or index of the book for whatever area you may need help with at the moment.

This book addresses different aspects of your divorce and does not need to be read completely to help you with certain areas. However, if you do not read the book from cover to cover, you may miss important information.

CHAPTER 1 - BEFORE DIVORCE

Planning Your Divorce Before Anyone Files

It is best to start planning your divorce weeks if not months before anyone actually files for divorce. In fact, many people do plan for a divorce before they are even married. They do that by preparing a pre-nuptial agreement. A pre-nuptial agreement is an agreement signed by the soon-to-be spouses that sets forth how assets and debts will be divided in the event of a divorce.

There is also something called a post-nuptial agreement, which is an agreement signed by a couple who is already married and who want to set forth what will happen in the event of a divorce. Post-nuptial agreements are often entered into when a couple is on the verge of a divorce, usually for financial reasons, but they want to try to work it out. For example, this sometimes this happens when a wife spends money irresponsibly and her husband does not want to be responsible for all the debt his wife incurs. Each state has its own laws for post-nuptials, so it is important to consult with an attorney in your area.

Unfortunately, not everyone gets the chance to enter into a pre-nuptial or post-nuptial agreement. Sometimes papers are filed before you can do any planning. But if you are able to plan, you should. I have never heard anyone say they regretted planning for divorce, but I have heard many people say that they regretted not planning for their divorce.

If you believe your soon-to-be-ex is fair and kind and you believe the divorce will be amicable and he just wants to mediate, that is great. Hopefully that is how it will turn out. You can hope for the best, but you should still plan for the worst. One of my favorite phrases is: You don't know who you married until you divorce him. This statement is extremely accurate. People usually act much different during divorce than they did during the marriage. Divorce often brings out the worst in people and the relationship will be like nothing you have ever known. If you were used to getting your way during the marriage, your spouse may suddenly start digging in. If you were able to make all the decisions for your children, this may be a very different outcome than you had anticipated.

What do you have to lose by planning? Nothing. What do you have to lose by not planning? Money may get moved or disappear altogether. Suddenly, your spouse who previously wanted nothing to do with the children will want them 50% of the time. Plan as much as possible.

Throughout this book I will provide tips, notes and examples for ease of reading and easy reference.

IMPORTANT
TIP #1

If you are already dating or involved with someone, do not let your soon to be ex know about any new significant other until the divorce is complete if at all possible. Nothing can interfere with an amicable divorce like a new boyfriend or girlfriend. Even if your soon to be ex has moved on and is dating, more times than not there will still be a bad reaction to you moving on.

When planning for a divorce, don't be vocal or dramatic about it. Your plan should be kept somewhat secret. You should not let your soon to be ex or your kids know that you are planning for divorce. If you want to tell your parents or your siblings, that is fine. But the fewer people you tell, the less likely your soon-to-be-ex will find out. It is not uncommon for confidants to tell your secret.

NOTE
Triggers that will interfere with your life/divorce

The following are triggers that are very likely to wreak havoc in your world before, during and or after your divorce.

1. Your ex learning that you have a new significant other.
2. Your ex seeing you with a new significant other for the first time.
3. Your ex finding out your kids met the new significant other for the first time.
4. Getting engaged.
5. Moving in with your new significant other.
6. Getting re-married
7. Getting pregnant or your new significant other getting pregnant.
8. Going on big vacations.
9. Your children telling the other parent how much fun they had with you.
10. Buying a new car.
11. Buying a new house.

You will need to make plans on either staying where you are living or finding a new place to live. This can be tricky. If you own the house or are on the lease of a house or apartment, you may not want your soon to be ex to continue to live with you. However, it is not always easy to get your soon to be ex to leave. You may need a court order, or you may need to evict your soon to be ex. But you need to have a plan. If your ex owns the home or is on the lease of the home or the apartment, you may need to find a new place to live. You should understand that choosing a place to live is important if you have one or more children. If you have children, you will need to find a place to live that is safe for your children. Your kids do not necessarily need to have their own rooms, but it is helpful. You should not move into a place where you have a roommate who drinks a lot or uses drugs. Keep in mind, your living situation will be scrutinized. You will also want to keep in mind the location of your new home and consider the distance between your ex's home and your child's school.

When planning for your divorce, you will also want to make plans for custody/legal decision-making/parenting time, if you have children; and you will want make plans to equally or equitably divide all marital assets and debt. Financial planning may include, but is not limited to, division of property, division of debt and possibly spousal maintenance. In order to make plans for division of assets and debts, you need to know what marital assets and debts exist. It is important to consider all assets when you start your planning. For instance, does your spouse own a business? Is the business part yours? Do you have an interest in it? Do either of you have a retirement or investments? Were they funded or added to during the marriage?

Custody/Legal Decision-Making/Parenting Time

It seems like more and more states are moving towards 50/50 parenting time as the norm. Even if you are the one who stayed home with the children, took the children to doctor appointments, helped with school work and the like, the courts still regularly order 50/50 parenting time. The presumption is that it is important for children to have meaningful relationships with both parents. Even if the other parent never bathed or fed or seemed to want to care for the child, the court may allow that parent to step up if he wants to.

Set your goals. What custody and parenting time do you want? Do you want 50/50 parenting time? More than 50% parenting time? Do you want sole legal decision-making? You need to have a clear understanding of what you want before you start prepping. Don't act like you want 50/50 parenting time if you don't. If your soon to be ex abuses drugs or alcohol or you or your child, you probably don't want 50/50 parenting time.

Also, do you want sole legal decision-making or are you okay with joint legal decision-making. Many courts like to order joint . . . but that does not mean there are not exceptions. You need to be prepared and you need to have a darn good reason for wanting sole legal decision-making.

When planning your divorce, you should take precautionary measures in order to obtain the legal decision-making authority and parenting time you want. Below are precautionary measures that will help you to obtain the best results.

Know your child

You should know things about your child that are important, such as what foods your child likes and what foods your child hates or is allergic to. You should also know things like your child's favorite color, activity, outfit, tv shows, games, etc. If you do not know your child, get to know your child.

You should also know your child's personality. Is your child shy or outgoing? Is your child messy or neat? Is your child afraid of heights or the dark or bugs? Does your child love animals? Is your child kind or selfish? Is your child religious? These are important things to know about your child.

Make sure you know the people who care for your child. You should know the names of doctors, dentists, teachers, tutors and even their friends and their friends' parents. Know if your child takes medications or is allergic to medications. Be involved in as much of your child's life as possible.

If you do not know all of that information, learn it. Ask questions and take notes if necessary. Kids love to communicate via text these days. If this is your child's preferred way of communicating, indulge it. However, you should be sure that you are being appropriate in your texts because we regularly see texts between children and parents used in court.

Don't send texts to your child trying to turn him against his father. Don't call your ex names or put her down in texts (or at all). I have seen children record their parents saying terrible things about the other parent. Assume that everything you say or write will be used in court.

Quality Time with Your Child

Make sure you spend quality time with your child. If you have an infant, you should be feeding, changing diapers, bathing and putting to bed. Develop your own bedtime ritual of bathing and reading stories. If your child is older, you should attend your child's games/sport activities, doctor, dentist appointments and school conferences, if possible, you should also be spending one on one time with your child(ren); help with homework, play catch, make slime, play a video game with him. The goal is to make sure you are really involved with your children. It's important to set up this relationship prior to you separating. You really want to have a good foundation with your child.

At some point during your divorce, your children may be interviewed. You would like them to have positive things to say about your relationship. It is up to you to make it a good relationship. It is not up to your child. I sometimes hear parents complain that their child isn't texting or calling. It is normal for kids not to want to be around their parents. It is your job to make sure you stay in your child's life. Maybe start a ritual, such as Sunday brunch with just you and your child or maybe weekly hiking or working out or shopping or ice cream.

Social media

Just say no to social media before and during the divorce or post decree action. Do not air your dirty laundry on social media. It will be used against you. Even if you believe you are being really slick by not using your ex's name, people will figure it out. And, if people can figure it out, the judge can figure it out.

Social media postings are often used against litigants. Even if your privacy settings are high and even if you have blocked your soon to be ex, she will inevitably have a friend who has a friend that is friends with you. Facebook posts are used against litigants every single day in court. Furthermore, the judge will not like it if your children have access to your postings and you are badmouthing the other parent or posting quotes or phrases that are clearly meant for your ex.

If you make a living using social media, be very careful about what you post. Do not post anything that can be taken as a slight against your ex. Do not air your dirty laundry. Do not post any pictures of you partying. Do not post any pictures of you smoking. Do not post any pictures of you breaking any laws. Do not post any pictures of your new significant other. Do not post any pictures of your children unless your ex has already approved and, if you do, make sure they are dressed appropriately and acting appropriately.

Do not post pictures of your teenager drinking alcohol or smoking/vaping. Don't "like" pictures of your adult child drinking, smoking pot, smoking/vaping or otherwise appearing as though they would be a bad influence on your minor children.

Smoking cigarettes

If you can quit, now would be a great time. Courts may use smoking and even vaping against you in court. I have seen courts limit parenting time of a smoking parent. If you are unable to stop smoke, do not smoke in your car when your child is with you. Do not smoke in your home. Do not smoke in front of your child. If your ex is smoking, get photos of him smoking near the child or smoking in the car with your child in there. Try not to make it obvious. You don't want your child see you trying to get your ex in trouble. Text or email your disapproval of him smoking around the child. This is especially important if your child has asthma and/or if you have been told to keep your child away from cigarette smoke. If your soon to be ex stops, great. If he tells you to mind your own business, then you will have memorialized that inappropriate behavior.

Drugs Use and Abuse

During your divorce, any drugs you use, either legally or illegally will be scrutinized. Even if you are obtaining drugs, such as pain killers or sleeping pills from your doctor, your use of prescription drugs will be looked over carefully.

For instance, if you are using sleeping pills to get to sleep, how will those affect your ability to parent? If you are using prescription oxycodone, or a similar drug, for back pain, your usage of them may become an issue. If you use in the morning, do you drive your child after using them? If you use at night, do you wake up early enough to get your child to school? When you use the drugs, how does your body react? Will your reaction to the drugs interfere with parenting time?

If you are using illegal drugs, stop as soon as possible. If you check yourself into a rehabilitation hospital you should know that those records will likely be subpoenaed. However, if you are going to be required to prove sobriety anyway, you may as well go. Just remember, it will be used against you in court.

It is important to know that even "legal" drugs can be misused or abused. Just because you have a prescription does not mean your use will not negatively impact your ability to parent and/or your case.

Marijuana is fully legal in many states and is available for medicinal purposes in other states. Know the law in your state so you will know whether or not you should completely stop using marijuana. As stated above, it is important to know that even if you have a "medical marijuana card" the court or an evaluator may still find that you are using marijuana for pleasure, not for medical purposes and/or abusing it. Just like drinking and driving, you should not be driving your child after using marijuana. You also should not be leaving marijuana edibles out in your children's reach. Lock up the marijuana, even if it is legal.

If your ex is using drugs and you are concerned with your ex's ability to coparent and parent appropriately, make sure you use specific facts when telling the court why you have a problem with him using drugs. Pictures of your ex partying while using marijuana might show that the marijuana was not being used medicinally but instead was used for fun.

Courts regularly order parents suspected of abusing drugs to submit to random drug tests. The testing facilities can test for drugs using urine, hair and fingernails/toenails. The hair can be taken from your head, armpit, legs, or pubic area.

Using a hair sample to test for drugs provides information for the past 90 days[2]. Using a fingernail/toenail sample for drug testing can provide proof for drug usage for up to 6 months. Using a urine sample for drug testing can provide feedback for the past three to four days, depending on the substance being tested for and the amount of drug used.

If you want to have your ex tested for drugs or alcohol, remember, these drug tests aren't fool proof. One search on the internet will provide you with substances that allegedly will help you pass all types of tests. The nail test might be the best choice, but not if your ex bites her nails or trims them low. If you have a good reason to suspect drug use but tests, come back negative, you may want to find proof that your ex purchased an item to use to help pass the test.

If a person ordered to take a drug test attempts to drink water to clear his urine of evidence of drug use, the test result may come up diluted. Courts will often count a diluted test as "positive".

Alcohol Use and Abuse

If you are using drugs and/or alcohol, be very careful. It is not uncommon for people to begin consuming more alcohol when they are going through a divorce. If you are on social media, I'm sure you have seen the memes about wine and day drinking bottles of alcohol. Unfortunately, drinking a bottle of wine a

---

[2] Hair follicle testing can pick up drugs past 90 days for heavy users.

night may not be appropriate and it may interfere with your ability to parent. Furthermore, it will be used against you if there is proof. Simply because alcohol is legal does not mean it can't be abused and that it will not be considered a problem by the court.

If you are an alcoholic or you are concerned that you may have a problem, you should quit immediately. Your children may also be asked if they have seen you drinking or if they have seen you drunk. They may be asked how often they see you using alcohol. Their words can go a long way to hurt your case. It is best to use alcohol minimally during your divorce.

If you suspect that your ex has an alcohol problem, you can ask that they submit to alcohol testing. Alcohol can be tested randomly through urine samples or through a breathalyzer device. There is a group called SoberLink that provides a breathalyzer that randomly generates test requirements and uploads them to the user account. If you are concerned for your child's safety, this might be the best bet. You should understand that consuming alcohol is not illegal, it is only when consuming alcohol interferes with a parent's ability to care for her child that it may become an issue the court will investigate.

As stated above, if a person tries to clear her system of drugs by drinking water, the test may come back as "diluted". If that is the case, the court may consider the test result "positive".

Domestic Violence

Domestic violence can be physical, emotional, coercive and even financial. If you are living together and you are being abused, call the police when it happens. If you are even thinking of splitting up, you need this evidence. Otherwise, the lack of evidence will be used against you. This is not the time to protect your ex. You should go to the hospital if you are hurt and you should take pictures of any cuts, bruises or destroyed property. So many times, we see women who have no records of their abuse because they always protected their spouse. If you are planning for a divorce, get the evidence of the abuse when it happens.

If there has been domestic violence in the past, get proof. Many judges are extremely skeptical when it comes to domestic violence accusations. Sadly, some people have lied about domestic violence claims, so judges want to be sure. If you have pictures of bruises, hospital records, police records, or damaged property, make sure to keep those safe. If you have emails or texts showing any other type of abuse, make sure you safeguard those. By safeguard, I mean email them to a friend so your ex cannot delete them.

To help prove abuse allegations, you can also use witness testimony if any observed the abuse, you can use recordings, and/or emails and texts where your ex has apologized to you for abusing you, or you have said something about the abuse to your ex and he did not deny the abuse. There is typically a "cycle" of abuse that is shown by abuse, abuse, denial, apology and promising not to do it again, periods of kindness, then build up then explosive anger again. You want to use facts and evidence to paint the picture of the cycle of abuse. Unfortunately, not all judges are educated on domestic violence. You may need to educate to your judge. You want to do that without making the judge feel stupid. If you can bring in an expert that would be great. Also, if you have a counselor who has diagnosed you with PTSD due to abuse, that might be helpful. See the table below, provided by: https://www.icadv.org.au/resources/.

Cycle of Domestic Violence

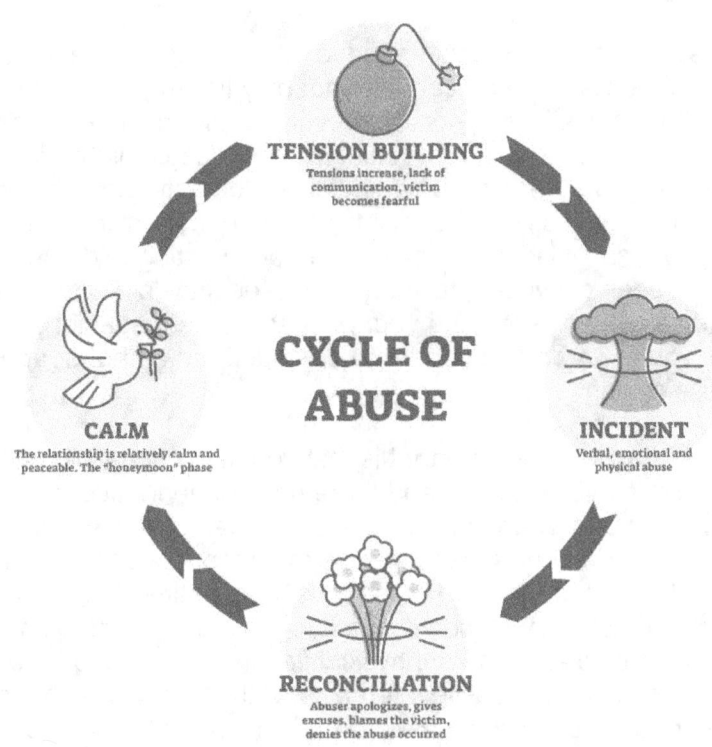

The cycle of violence diagram (above) really helps to put into perspective the different phases of domestic violence. This table may also help to jog your memory of the cycle of abuse you suffered. It may be helpful to for you create a timeline of abuse or memorialize it in a calendar or journal so you can keep track of it. You want to be able to provide the court with real facts. However, keep in mind, if you want to use one page of a calendar or journal, you will likely be required to disclose the entire journal. So be sure to only write in the journal what you are willing to have shared with your ex and the court.

There are also books about how domestic violence affects children and how to help children heal from domestic violence. It may be helpful to get one or more of the books to help guide you through this difficult time.

If you are being wrongfully accused of abusing your spouse, or you think fights. Leave the premises if a fight begins. Walk away from arguments. Do not put threats in writing. Document your ex's erratic behavior either by recording her or following up with email or text communication. It is important to know your recording laws in your state. It is probably best to not be drinking if drinking causes you to engage in fights.

If you have been abusive, you need to stop immediately and get help if necessary. There are classes you can take not only for anger management but also specifically for domestic violence. However, you should talk to an attorney prior to taking any classes to see how taking those classes might affect your court case. If you believe there will be a finding of domestic violence or there is a criminal conviction or admission of domestic violence then taking the classes should not hurt your case. However, if you are not admitting to domestic violence and you have not been convicted, taking the classes may look like an admission. However, if you take the classes and your ex tries to use it against you, you can simply say that you are always on board to do better and be better and you thought the class couldn't hurt.

One thing that is really important is that you may need to "plead the fifth". If there has been domestic violence and there has not been a confession or a conviction, anything you say can and will be used against you. So, if you testify in family court that your husband took money from your purse so you grabbed a glass and threw it at him and hit him in the face, that testimony will likely be used in criminal court and you may be convicted. It is really important to speak with an attorney before admitting any kind of physical fighting. If you plead the fifth in civil court, the court can make a negative inference for the family case or civil case, however, you cannot be convicted based on "taking the fifth". So, make sure to talk to an attorney if there was domestic violence.

> **IMPORTANT**
> **TIP #2**
>
> <u>Safeguard Evidence</u> - Evidence is documents, pictures, and/or recordings that you provide to the judge to back up what you are saying. I cannot tell you how many times I have had clients come to me for a consultation and say their ex took their phone and erased everything. Make sure you safeguard it. Send it to a friend or family member. Upload it to a cloud or email that you are certain is secure. Make copies and give them to people. Or do all of the above. If it you end up in court with no evidence, it will be he said - she said and the judge will not know who to believe. Evidence is important.

Financial Issues

Typically, married couples acquire assets and debt during the course of their marriage. If you are in a community property state, they are joint. If you are not in a community property state, they may or may not be joint. It may depend on how the items are titled. When planning for a divorce, it is important to know what assets and debts have been acquired during marriage. It is helpful to do an inventory

<u>Inventory</u>

An inventory is a list of all the assets and debts that were acquired during the marriage. With each item in the list, you should try to provide a description of the property, the date it was acquired, the purchase price, the current value, any amount owed on the property and the net value, along with who should have the property. It is helpful if you put this on an Excel Spreadsheet for ease of reading and to ensure all property and debt is accounted for and values have been equally or equitably divided. You can also leave sections blank if you do not know the information.

EXAMPLE:

Desc	Date of Purch	Purch value	Current Value	Amt Owed	Net Value	H	W	Notes
Home	1/15/12	$200,000	$250,000	$90K	$160K	$80K	$80K	SELL
Land	8/10/10	$40K	$75K	0	$75K	$75k	0	
Chase #1122	7/7/07	NA	$25,376		$25,376		$25,376	
Retire-ment			$380K			$190k	$190K	
Wife's Bus.			$185K				$185K	
Jeep	3/14/19	$28K	$25K	Unkn will suppl	unkn	unkn		

Personal Property

 Personal Property is "movable property" and does not include land or buildings. You will want to take an inventory of everything prior to filing, before things disappear. When couples split, personal property inevitably disappears.

 Whether you own or rent your home, you likely furnished it with your ex. You will need to take an inventory of everything in the house. You should do this before anyone moves out and/or removes anything from the home. Taking pictures or videos work great for a quick home inventory and you can go through them later to create a written inventory. If you or your ex had furnishings before marriage and brought those furnishings into the house, whoever had those furnishings prior to marriage still owns the property. For instance, if you joined two completely furnished households together and your husband brought his couches, that he had owned before the marriage, those are still his couches. The same is true for each party's pre-marital furnishings.

 You may also want to provide values for each item to make it easier to divide assets equitably. Each party should end up with approximately the same total value when complete.

Property	Craig's List Value	Husband	Wife	Notes
Mountain Bike	$300	$300		
Pool Table	$800	$800		
Master Bedroom Set	$1,500		$1,500	
Guest Room Bedroom Set (Bed, 2 night stands, Dresser)	$500	$500		
Living Room Set (2 couches, 2 side tables, coffee table)	$400		$400	
Dining Room Table plus 6 chairs	$300	$300		
Total	$3,800	$1,900	$1,900	

Real Property

You will want to be sure to list *all* the real properties your and or your ex own. This should include the marital home, a second home, rental properties, land, property owned by a business and the like. Even if the property is titled in just one parties' name, both parties may still have an interest in the home. Do not be bullied by a spouse who says it is all hers because it is in her name. It would be worth consulting with a lawyer in your area to determine what your rights are.

While you are doing this investigating and preparing for your divorce, try to get copies of the titles of your properties and the loan information. You can likely find copies of the titles and purchase prices online. You will also want to know the how much the current mortgage balances are and the current value of the properties. Having those values will help you determine the equity in the properties. Knowing the equity in the properties will better help you divide assets.

Determining the current value of the properties can be done by having the property appraised or obtain a broker's analysis. You may also find some values on Zillow; however, the accuracy of Zillow is regularly questioned, but it is better than simply guessing.

If there have been any improvements done on the properties, such as a remodel, or adding a pool, or adding additions, you should gather all receipts and invoices. It would be helpful for you to have information on how those improvements were paid for. For instance, if your home is your ex's sole and separate property, it is important to know how much marital income was put into the property to determine if you have an equitable interest in the property.

If the improvements to the property were paid for with an equity loan and the equity loan was repaid with marital funds, that may also give you a claim to an equitable interest in the property.

If your ex had a property prior to marriage, but continued to pay the mortgage during the marriage, that also might cause you to have an equitable interest.

Vehicles/Boats/RVs/Motorcycles/Jet Skis/Snow Mobiles/Quads

You will want to be sure to have an inventory of all vehicles and the approximate values. You can find the values of many of the above items on Kelly Blue Book or NADA or Boat Value.

Bank Accounts

Make copies of at least the last six months of bank statements if you can. If you believe money is missing, you should go back a couple of years to see if you can find it. You should also add all the accounts to the above inventory. If you believe money has wrongfully disappeared, be sure to prepare a spreadsheet showing the money transfers or any issues that you have.

Retirement, Pensions, Stocks and Investment Accounts

Make copies of statements from any retirement accounts you may have. This should include all 401Ks, any stocks or bonds, any investment accounts. You will want the value of the account from the date you file for divorce. Each state has different dates they look at when determining when to end the marital community. To be safe, have at least six months of statements. Again, if you feel there has been any misappropriation of funds, you may want to have two or more years of statements so you can trace where the money went.

Also, if you had money in your retirement prior to marriage, be sure to get the statements from before marriage if possible. That will show what amount was in the retirement account before marriage, which the court will probably find to be your separate property portion of the retirement account. However, this is an era where legal advice in your specific jurisdiction will be helpful.

Pensions can be very tricky to determine the value. You may need to hire a forensic accountant to determine the present value of a pension. You may have significant rights to a pension that you do not want to give up.

Businesses

When businesses are started during the marriage, the value of that business will be considered at the time of divorce. If you are in a community property state, it will be community property unless you or your spouse signed away any rights to it. If you are in an equitable distribution state, there will be an equitable division, unless again, if either party has waived any rights to it or either party

Health insurance

Get copies of your health insurance coverage. You will want to know the monthly insurance costs. If you cannot get those before someone files for divorce, then make sure you get them afterwards. Health insurance expenses are often considered in both child support calculations and spousal maintenance calculations. These numbers are important.

Life Insurance

You will want to get copies of your life insurance. If it is term life insurance you will really just need a copy of the bill. Although term life insurance can have some value, it is difficult to value term life insurance and often not considered an asset to be divided. On the other hand, whole life insurance does have a surrender value and is much easier to value.

Debt

You will want to know want to know what debt is outstanding for a couple of reasons. First, depending on your situation, you may want to pay the debt off or pay it down. Or, you may want to keep it there. Debt can have an effect on spousal maintenance and the division of assets. Second, you will also want to be sure that all debt is accounted for. The best way to do this is to get copies of credit reports to ensure neither party has any debt that is not accounted for in the decree.

Home Equity Loans

There may be a Home Equity Loan or HELOC which means if you own your marital residence, that residence may have been used to secure a loan which you may have obtained from your bank. It is important to know if there is a HELOC and what the money was used for. You may also want to know if it was taken out in lump sum or it was in the form of a "line of credit". If it was a line of credit type loan you should try to determine when "loans" from the line of credit occurred and, if possible, what the money was used for.

No matter how the loan was taken, you may want to trace where the money went. This may be important if one of you keep the home. For instance, if you obtained the loan so you could remodel the home, the loan should probably go with the house. However, if you took the loan and paid off a vehicle or student loan or used it for living expenses, then the loan might need to be divided another way.

You may want to create a table.

Date	Amount	Purchase
2/22/21	$55,000	Added pool to backyard
2/25/21	$2,000	Trash removal from backyard
3/2/21	$15,600	Paid of credit cards

In this example, $57,000 of the HELOC debt should go with the house, however, $15,600 may be better suited to be equitably divided between the parties unless that credit card was also used for home improvements. If that is the case, then maybe the entire debt of the HELOC goes with the house.

Rental/Lease agreements

There may be lease/rental agreements for cars or homes. They may be important when dividing up expenses, determining spousal maintenance, or dividing assets or debts. For instance, if there is a lease for a home, but the lease does not expire for 3 years, one party will either be required to live there or you may end up breaking the lease. It is important to know your options and also important to know for you to plan for a new place to live or a new vehicle to drive.

Car titles

Like real property titles, they may be important when determining distribution of assets. If you can get possession of the titles, you should. It doesn't necessarily affect the outcome of who ends up with the vehicle(s) but if you are required to sell a vehicle, it will make your life easier. They may also help you get a Kelly Blue Book value on the vehicle.

> **NOTE**
> If your vehicle is in your soon to be ex's name, try to get it in your name or get your name added to the title. I have seen people call the police and report their cars stolen in an attempt to get their ex arrested. If there is any way to get that car in your name before separation, you should try to do so.

Stocks

If you have any information on stocks owned or actual certificates, be sure to make copies of those. If you have any information, such as an offer letter, on how and when company stocks may vest, get that too. This can be important in determining the value of the stock and if they are part of the marital assets to be divided.

> **EXAMPLE**
> If your employer gives you stock in the company when you are hired, but they do not vest until you have worked there for 5 years, those may not all be part of the marital assets. Each state may have different rules about that and you should speak with an attorney in your area to determine if the stock options are part of the marital property.

Credit cards

If you have a spouse that is racking up debt on your joint credit cards, you may want to cancel the cards. If you cannot cancel the cards because you are not the primary card holder, you may want to write a letter to the credit card company and let them know that you are no longer willing to be responsible for any new debt associated with the card. It may or may not work, but at least you have attempted to give notice.

Assume that once you either ask for a divorce or file papers that your credit cards will be cancelled and your bank accounts will be emptied.

New Bank Account

Set up a new bank account. You will need to disclose it, but you should have it ready for when you file the papers and get a credit card in your name only. Your credit will likely go down during the divorce, so you want to have a credit card available.

Prenuptial Agreement

Prenuptial Agreements are agreements signed prior to marriage that help to guide how assets and debts will be distributed in the event of a divorce. If you signed a prenuptial agreement, find it. Review it. Take it to an attorney to determine the validity of it. If you do not dispute the Agreement, then it should set out, for the most part, how assets and debts will be divided.

However, even if you have a prenuptial agreement, you may still need to make tables and gather documents. Because the prenuptial agreement may only address separate property or property acquired before marriage. You may want to talk to an attorney before going through all your records and making all the tables of assets and debt.

Post-Nuptial Agreement

A post-nuptial agreement is an agreement between a husband and wife that is signed after marriage. Parties sometimes enter into these agreements when financial issues are causing a strain on the marriage.

If you have signed a post-nuptial agreement, check with an attorney to determine the validity of the agreement.

Employment

If you or your soon-to-be ex received a contract for employment, be sure to have a copy of that contract. The contract may have information about wages, bonuses, stock options and the like.

Loans

If you borrowed money from anyone, especially a family member, make sure you have a contract of some sort and proof that repayment is required. (Again, you may need to speak with an attorney in your area to determine what makes a contract "enforceable" and then make sure it complies with those requirements.) If you do not have proof, the court may not believe that repayment is required and you may be stuck with a debt. Furthermore, even if you do have proof, the court may not believe it. Therefore, the person who loaned you money may be required to testify about the expected repayment.

> **EXAMPLE**
> Your parents' loan you $50,000 for a down payment on a house. You are supposed to repay the loan when you are able to refinance the house or when it sells. However, in court, your ex says that it was a gift and that no repayment is required. If you do not have proof that it was a "loan" and not a "gift" then you may be stuck with the debt.

CHAPTER 2 - PROCEDURES – RULES – STATUTES

When you are involved in a court case, you are required to know all the rules, procedures and statutes, just as if you were an attorney. You may have heard that old phrase *ignorance of the law is not an excuse*. You may get a judge that will give you some leeway, but I believe those judges are few and far between. In this case, ignorance is not bliss.

Most states and counties have their court rules and procedures online and they are easily accessible. Many courts have a library and a self-help service to help guide you. Take advantage of any free resources you can get. Often times, if you are kind, friendly and humble, you can get help from people at the Court. Make sure you are not demanding or demeaning to anyone at the Court. Court staff talk to each other. Judicial assistants speak with clerks and judges. If you are a jerk to the clerk or judicial assistant, the judge will probably hear about it. Likewise, if you are kind and friendly, the staff may also inform the judge about that.

STATUTES

Each state has a set of statutes. Statutes are the laws of the state and they are created by the legislature. These laws will provide factors the court will need to consider in order for them to make informed decisions. You should consider this your playbook.

> **EXAMPLE:**
> **Arizona Revised Statute 25-403**
>
> *25-403. Legal decision-making; best interests of child*
> A. The court shall determine legal decision-making and parenting time, either originally or on petition for modification, in accordance with the best interests of the child. The court shall consider all factors that are relevant to the child's physical and emotional well-being, including:
> 1. The past, present and potential future relationship between the parent and the child.
> 2. The interaction and interrelationship of the child with the child's parent or parents, the child's siblings and any other person who may significantly affect the child's best interest.
> 3. The child's adjustment to home, school and community.
> 4. If the child is of suitable age and maturity, the wishes of the child as to legal decision-making and parenting time.
> 5. The mental and physical health of all individuals involved.
> 6. Which parent is more likely to allow the child frequent, meaningful and continuing contact with the other parent. This paragraph does not apply if the court determines that a parent is acting in good faith to protect the child from witnessing an act of domestic violence or being a victim of domestic violence or child abuse.
> 7. Whether one parent intentionally misled the court to cause an unnecessary delay, to increase the cost of litigation or to persuade the court to give a legal decision-making or a parenting time preference to that parent.
> 8. Whether there has been domestic violence or child abuse pursuant to section 25-403.03.
> 9. The nature and extent of coercion or duress used by a parent in obtaining an agreement regarding legal decision-making or parenting time.
> 10. Whether a parent has complied with chapter 3, article 5 of this title.
> 11. Whether either parent was convicted of an act of false reporting of child abuse or neglect under section 13-2907.02.
>
> B. In a contested legal decision-making or parenting time case, the court shall make specific findings on the record about all relevant factors and the reasons for which the decision is in the best interests of the child.
> Eff. 2021

When you are preparing your case, try to provide evidence for each factor. For instance, when preparing for factor one "The past, present and potential future relationship between the parent and the child" you will want to make sure you provide facts that show the great relationship you had in the past with the child, the relationship you currently have with your child and the relationship you plan to have in the future. This is where you would say something like you have been involved in every aspect of your child's life. You have attended doctor appointments, school conferences, you bathed the child when he was little and you changed diapers etc. Let the court know how involved you are and what your plans are for future involvement. Again, do this for every factor. And make sure you provide facts.

In this case, the second factor is "The interaction and interrelationship of the child with the child's parent or parents, the child's siblings and any other person who may significantly affect the child's best interest". If the child has half/step siblings or aunts, uncles and/or grandparents that are a part of the child's life, make sure you let the court know about those relationships. For instance, if your daughter visits with your parents every Sunday for brunch, that would be important for the court to know. If the child does not have a close relationship with any extended family members, maybe now is the time to build a relationship.

Rules of Procedures

Rules of Procedure are different than Statutes. States, counties and even cities have rules and procedures for their courts. Those rules are typically created by the court. You will be expected to know all the rules of the court in which you are appearing and filing for your divorce. These rules will give you information about procedures for filing petitions and motions, along with information about deadlines for responses and replies, and discovery and disclosure. Missing a deadline can get your whole case thrown out. It is important to know these rules. It is also very important to be timely. You should be able to find your court rules online.

> **EXAMPLE**
>
> All states have statutes about divorce similar to above, but when you file for divorce, you must follow the Rules of Procedure while keeping in mind that each county may have their own "local rules" that you also must follow.

In Arizona, you would need to file a Petition for Dissolution, Separation or Paternity. The *statutes* would be responsible for what information you put in the Petition. The rules of procedure would require you to make four copies; one for you, one for the judge, one for the court and one for the opposing party. You will likely be required to pay a fee to file the petition, however some states and or counties will allow for a deferral of payment or may waive them if you can prove you are unable to pay. Many jurisdictions will have those rules online.

Statutes will also control what documents you file. For instance, if you are married, you will file a Petition for Dissolution. If you are not married but have a child together, you would need to file a Petition to Establish Paternity. If you want child support, or certain parenting time you would need to ask for that too. A Judge can only give the relief requested. Therefore, if you don't petition for parenting time, the judge may not be able to give you parenting time.

Are You Legally Married?

The first thing you need to know is if you are legally married. If you are legally married, you would file for divorce in family court. Marriage is a legal union between two people, so you must determine if you are indeed married If you are not legally married, but you have children in common, you will need to file for paternity. However, if you are not legally married but you have purchased property together and do not have children together, you may need to file documents and seek relief in a different court. Some counties are very small and may have one court and even one judge that does everything.

Common Law Marriage

A common law marriage is a marriage where two people live together and hold themselves out as married. Common law marriages are only recognized in 12 states (at the time of writing this book). If you believe you are married, via common law marriage, check your state to see if it recognizes common law marriages.

Gay marriages

Gay marriages are valid in all 50 states now. Some issues may arise as to the length of the marriage, just make sure to check your state's statutes.

Covenant marriages (only done in very few states)

A covenant marriage is a marriage where the parties agree to pre-marital counseling and restrictions on divorce. If you have a covenant marriage, be sure to check your state's statutes to be sure you meet the requirements to proceed with divorce.

Conventional Marriage

A conventional marriage is a marriage that is common in your area. In the United States, that is a marriage between a man and a woman.

Voidable Marriage

A voidable marriage is a marriage that can be voided under the State's law if one or both parties want the marriage to be voided.

Invalid Marriage/Void Marriage

There are a couple of things that can make a marriage invalid.

1. Bigamy/polygamy is not valid in the US. If you or your spouse were still married to another person when you married each other, your marriage is void and can be annulled.

2. If a child is underage at the time of marriage without a valid parents' approval, the marriage may not be valid. Check the statutes in your area.

If you thought you were married, but weren't and you bought a house together or acquired debt together, you may be required to bring your case in civil court and not family court. This is especially important when you are hiring an attorney. Many family law attorneys do not practice civil law. The rules may be significantly different.

You Are Not Married, But You Have a Child Together

If you are not married but have at least one child together, you will need to file for paternity instead of divorce. Filing for paternity will still allow you to set up custody, a parenting plan and child support.

Property Acquired Before Marriage

Property Acquired before marriage may be treated differently than property acquired during your marriage. You should consult an attorney in your area to help you with this possibly complex issue. Some courts may treat it the same as if it was purchased during the marriage if it appears the parties meant for the property to be marital property. Other courts may treat the property as either party's separate property.

CHAPTER 3 - BEGINNING THE PROCESS

Separating/Moving out

You may have heard that it if you leave the marital home, it is difficult for you to get back into it. That can definitely be true. Remember, everyone's facts are different. No two cases that are identical. But courts often like to keep the status quo. Therefore, if you have moved out and you have a new place to live, the court may want to keep it that way. However, it is not written in stone and if you moved out for good cause, then you may be able to ask the court to let you move back in and make the other party move out. If you do this, make sure you request a specific date to have the other party move out. Also be specific about what furniture stays and what furniture can be removed by the other party.

Hiring Someone to Help with the Divorce

<u>Professionals Available to Help with Divorce</u>

There are many professionals who can help you with your divorce.

<u>Do I Need an Attorney?</u>

If you have significant assets/debt or if you have children, I believe that you should at least consult with a lawyer prior to divorcing. You should do this for several reasons. First, the lawyer has likely helped with many more divorces that you and has experience that can prove invaluable. This can be important when setting up parenting plans and knowing what issues may be problematic. Second, a lawyer would know the specific laws in your region and help you understand how to get what you want. Third, your lawyer will know what you are entitled to when it comes to tricky assets such as businesses, stocks, pensions and the like.

That being said, if you have a simple divorce and you are able to work with your ex, and you don't have many assets or debts, then maybe you don't need to speak with an attorney.

Just don't get pressured by your ex to give up things that are valuable. If you do, you will likely have "buyer's remorse", meaning you will be upset about giving everything up later. This is very common with pensions and retirements. Sometimes one party will guilt the other party into agreeing to let her keep the retirement. However, in 10 years you may really need that retirement. The courts have rules to determine what is fair, just follow those and don't be talked into giving up something of value.

If you are going to see a lawyer, it is best to get a referral from a friend. I once had a client's ex refer a client to me. I think it was the best referral I ever received because it showed that I wasn't a jerk to him, but I was good at what I did. The ex referred the person to me instead of to his own lawyer.

How to Choose an Attorney

Choosing an attorney that is right for you is important. You should interview a couple of different attorneys to make sure you find one that you click with. If you are the type of person who wants to be kept in the loop on everything, let the attorney know. If you are the type who wants to bury your head in the sand, also let your attorney know that too.

Ask the attorney what to expect as far as responsiveness you email and phone calls. Some attorneys are great at getting back to you and some are not.

If you are a victim of domestic violence, be sure to find an attorney who takes that seriously and who will stand up for you if your ex starts to bully you.

Legal Paraprofessionals

A couple states permit legal paraprofessionals to practice law. They are not required to go to law school but they do have to meet other requirements. Allowing paraprofessionals to represent people is an attempt to help people who are unable to afford an attorney.

At the time of writing this book, Arizona allows paraprofessionals to practice in specific areas of law after meeting significant requirements. Other states have permitted them in the past and have stopped permitting future paraprofessionals.

Certified Document Preparer

Certified document preparers can help self-represented litigants file their papers in some states. They may also be able to point you in the right direction for other help you may need.

Preparing Documents

Petitions for Dissolution / Annulment / Separation / Paternity

To get your case started you will need to file a petition. A petition is defined as a formal written request. Each state has their own rules for filing petitions.

When you prepare your petition, you will need to follow the requirements of your jurisdiction. You must state exactly what you are asking for in the title. For example: *Petition for Dissolution of Marriage with Children.* You may need to state your name, birthday, employer, length of time residing in the state, along with your requests for custody, child support, division of assets, division of debt, spousal maintenance, attorney fees, or anything else. If you do not specifically request what you want in your petition, the court may be precluded from granting your request. You may also be required to identify your children by name and date of birth.

Jurisdiction

Jurisdiction gives the Court power to make decisions in your case. If the Court does not have jurisdiction over you or the subject matter, that means they cannot make orders in your case. Courts get their jurisdiction from laws/statutes and rules. If there is not a rule giving the court power, they do not have power. Typically, if you and your spouse live in the same state for the required amount of time, the family court will have jurisdiction over you both.

All states have the power to set their jurisdictional requirements. For example, a party must live in Arizona at least 90 days prior to filing for divorce for the court to have jurisdiction over them. However, a child must live in the state for six months. Arizona follows the Uniform Child Custody Jurisdiction and Enforcement Act (UCCJEA.)

You can usually go online or go to a document preparer to fill out all the paperwork. Many states and counties have free services available both online and in person to help guide you through the divorce process. Make sure you are accurate and honest when you are filling out the papers. Remember, when you fill out the papers you are swearing that all the information is true and correct. If you try to hide anything it can be used against you if the truth is discovered.

Changing the Judge

Once you have filed all your papers, you will be given a case number and your case will likely be assigned to a judge. Some jurisdictions permit a change of judge without cause. However, more jurisdictions require a reason to change a judge. Check your local rules for changing judges.

If your jurisdiction does not require cause to change a judge, then just file a Notice of Change of Judge pursuant to your court rules.

If your jurisdiction does require cause to change a judge, list the rule and provide the specific reasons to change your judge. If your local rules require cause to change a judge, make sure you look up what would qualify for cause in your area. If the judge knows you, that might be cause. If the has a known and provable bias about a part of your case, that might work too. But you will need cause and you will need proof that the judge meets the criteria to be removed. If you are unable to prove the allegations, do not file to have the judge removed. Filing a document calling a judge biased or saying bad things about the judge will not help your case.

Setting Up Your Case

Whether you or your ex have filed, there is still time to work on setting up your case.

TIP #3

You should be taking every opportunity you can to build up evidence against your ex during this time. If you can get your ex to admit child abuse, domestic violence, alcohol or drug abuse, try to get it in writing - either in a text or email.

> **TIP #4**
>
> Ask for what you want and act like you want what you said you want.

I have had many clients swear to me that they want the other parent involved in their child's life and they want to co-parent with them. Then they spend the next hours spewing their hatred toward their ex and saying how horrible of a parent their ex is. Why on earth would anyone want their child to be around such a horrible person. Why would anyone want to co-parent with such a horrible person? The answer to both is they wouldn't. If what you really mean is that you want your ex to act normal and healthy and be a good parent, THEN when that happens you want to co-parent and you want your ex to participate in the child's life. Be specific about what you want.

In order to prepare your case for trial, if you are not already doing the items listed below, you need to start.

Start Caring for your children regularly and often. This means you should attend doctor/dental appointments and school conferences. You should attend your children's extra-curricular activities and games and show interest in what they are doing. If the children are at an age where you can help with homework, you should do so.

Take time to talk to your children and play games with them. Do not make excuses for not participating in your child's life otherwise those excuses may be the reason you are not granted the parenting time you want.

Domestic Violence

Each state may have their own definition of domestic violence. Domestic violence may include, but is not limited to, choking, hitting, kicking, pulling hair, pushing, grabbing, spitting on, threatening, yelling, chasing, harassing, restraining, destruction of property, name calling and the like. If someone is doing any of these to you, you are a victim of domestic violence. If you are doing these things to anyone, you are an abuser.

Victims of Domestic Violence

If you are a victim of domestic violence, it is important to have a plan and to keep yourself and your child safe. If you can safely document and/or memorialize any domestic violence, do so. Keep copies of text messages and emails that may show any wrongdoing. Take pictures of bruises or holes in the walls or broken property. If your ex hits you/lays hands on you, punches a wall, restrains you from leaving - call the police. Make a record of it. If you are injured, go to the hospital and tell them the truth about what happened. Do not lie to protect your ex and make sure to press charges if you can*. If you can get your ex to admit the domestic violence or if you can get them to apologize, either via email or text that would be helpful evidence. If they apologize on the phone or in person you may want to record them. [Footnote - laws about recording on phones and in person] Also, be sure to file an Order of Protection/Restraining Order. [INSERT FOOTNOTE - *If you ex will be fired from his job because of the DV charge, make sure you understand the repercussions. If you ex is fired, he will have a difficult time paying child support]

TIP #5

Do not fake domestic violence. If the judge determines that you did, you will no longer be a credible witness.

Domestic Violence Abusers

If you are currently being abusive or have been abusive in the past, **stop now**. If your soon to be ex tries to bait you into admitting it do not respond. You should consult an attorney to discuss any allegations of domestic violence and how to proceed. Each case is different.

Benefits of Taking an Anger Management or Domestic Violence Class	Possible issues with taking an Anger Management or Domestic Violence Class
1. You get the help you need. 2. Judges like when parents take an initiative to better themselves. 3. Get a head start on treatment if it is required for parenting time.	1. You may not be a candidate for a class, so talk to your attorney. 2. May look like an admission of guilt 3. Records can be subpoenaed. 4. Court may not require it.

You need to assume that everything you do or say will be either video or audio recorded and provided to the court. You need to assume every email and text you write will be shown to the judge.

It is sometimes a good idea to take the initiative and either take an anger management class or a domestic violence abuser class if you believe the other party can prove you committed domestic.

Involving Children

Do not involve your children in the upcoming divorce. Do not confide in your child about thoughts of divorce. This will unnecessarily put them in the middle and if they are interviewed by the Court, that information will likely be discovered and used against you in court. Judges do not like it when parents involve their kids in divorce. If your ex cheated on you, your kids do not need to know. They may know because they were present during fighting, however, you should not discuss it with them. This is a grown-up issue for the grownups to handle. The kids should be allowed to love both parents.

Assume that anything you text, email, write or speak will be used against you. If you text anything to your ex, assume it will be used in court. If you are screaming at your ex, assume you are being recorded and the video will be used to show how unstable you are. This is especially true if you are going crazy in front of the child. Make sure you keep your composure at this time, especially in front of the kids.

If you are going to counseling, remember, anything you say in counseling may be subject to discovery. That means your ex may subpoena all the counseling records and use them against you. However, if you are in counseling with your ex and you get him or her to admit to inappropriate behavior, you can use that against him/her.

Trying To Negotiate a Settlement Before Filing or Immediately Thereafter.

Some people try to have their case completely settled even before papers are filed. Some parties even fill out the papers together ahead of time. If you have minimal money, low debt, few assets and no kids go ahead and negotiate before filing. However, if you have some assets, maybe some retirement, kids and or debt, it could not hurt you to at least consult with a lawyer before agreeing to anything so you know your rights.

It seems like every time I have seen people try to get everything settled in a hurry, it turns out bad. Ask yourself, what's the rush? If you want to do it right, make sure you take the time to do it correctly. It also seems like the person pushing for a quick agreement is trying to pull a fast one and get away with something. It usually has to do with money . . . either a pension or child support. Often times one person will bully the other person to get documents signed. This frequently happens in cases that involve domestic violence where one parent threatens to take the child from the other if they go to court. Again, you are allowed to make bad deals, but you should really speak with a lawyer before you give everything away.

Also, make sure you research parenting plans to ensure you pick out a plan that is in the best interest of the child for the child's current age. For instance, a 3-month-old baby should not be on a week on week off schedule or they may have problems down the line. Parenting plans are addressed in further detail below.

CHAPTER 4 – ORDERS OF PROTECTION / RESTRAINING ORDER / INJUNCTIONS

There are different legal terms for the act of protecting oneself from another person. In Arizona, Orders of Protection are what you obtain to keep away a family member or someone with whom you have had a romantic relationship. Injunctions Against Harassment are used when you want to keep away someone who is not covered by the Order of Protection. Some jurisdictions use Restraining Orders for all protective orders. If your court has a self-help service, or a domestic violence help center, they will usually help you determine what type of order is needed. If a police officer is involved, he may also be able to point you in the right direction.

For purposes of this book, I will refer to domestic relation protective orders and Orders of Protections as OOPs.

Purpose of Order

The purpose of an OOP is to make someone stay away from someone else. It's really that simple. If you obtain an OOP against someone, that means you do not want them to be near you.

The OOP may also set parameters by which parties can communicate. For instance, if you get an OOP against your wife, it may say that she can only contact you via email or text. It may say she can contact you via phone.

The OOP may also require a party to surrender any guns in his possession. The OOP may permit one party to have exclusive use of the home. The OOP may also keep the defendant away from other addresses or even other people, such as children.

If an OOP prohibits contact from the defendant and his children, the court may have the ability to work around that order.

Another important purpose of an OOP is to put law enforcement on notice. If you have an OOP and the defendant breaks it and shows up, when you contact the police, be sure to let them know that you have an OOP and that you are afraid for your safety. When an OOP is in place, police will often take the call more seriously and react more quickly.

Sworn Testimony/Ex-Parte Hearing to Receive Order

To obtain an OOP, the person seeking the order (plaintiff) will be required to give some testimony either in writing or in person to a judge, a commissioner, or a magistrate. If the judge does not require the other party to appear or even have notice, the is called an ex-parte order. The testimony will need to convince the judge that domestic violence has occurred or is likely to occur. Each jurisdiction has different requirements; however, OOPs are usually not granted unless someone has a valid complaint.

Contested Hearing Before Order

A contested hearing before the OOP is granted means that you will be required to provide your ex with notice of the request for an OOP and you will be required to prove to the court that you need an order to protect you from your ex.

As with any hearing, you need to make sure you are prepared. The court will want evidence to prove what you say is true. You want to be calm to some extent, but you also may want to show fear and probably a little sadness. Screaming and freaking out will not help your case.

If you have any photos of bruises, or damaged property you will want to bring those to court. If you have police records or hospital records that discuss any abuse or problems with your ex, you will want to provide those too. If you have an audio/video recording that depicts your ex being violent or abusive, you should provide that too. Finally, if you know of someone who witnessed the abuse or threats and that person is willing to testify, you should have that person come to court.

Although OOP hearings are different than divorce trials and usually have different trial rules, you should be as prepared as you would for your divorce trial.

Contested Hearing After Order

If an order is granted after an ex-parte hearing, the court may permit the defendant to have a hearing in an attempt to quash the order. Both parties should prepare for this hearing as they would any other hearing and as stated above.

In Arizona, and I'm sure in other jurisdictions, it is not always the best idea to request a hearing. If the court upholds the OOP, the defendant could be stuck with the ruling for a year. If the children are on the OOP, that could affect the defendant's parenting time for up to a year.

NOTE

It is EXTREMELY important for a defendant, and maybe even the plaintiff in some cases, to speak to a criminal law attorney prior to testifying in an order of protection hearing. It is important to understand that anything said in ANY hearing can be used in a different hearing, such as a criminal hearing. If any party admits to hitting or pushing someone, they may be at risk of being convicted of a crime. Therefore, before either party says something incriminating, they should speak to a criminal lawyer in their area.

Upheld Order

If the order is upheld after a hearing, the defendant is bound by it for up to a year, or maybe more depending on the jurisdiction. The judge may modify if she finds cause.

Effect of Order on Family Case

Your order of protection may or may not have an effect on your family law case. Some family courts are willing to interfere with the order, some are not. You will need to check your jurisdiction.

Quashed Order

If your OOP gets quashed, that means the order is no longer in place and there are no longer restrictions on your ex.

Expiration of Order

If you have a valid OOP that is set to expire, check your local rules to see if you can extend the order. You may need to tell the judge why you need to extend the order. Good reasons to extend the order would be if your ex has violated the order or if you are still fearful, or if he has told people that he intends to hurt you or harass you.

CHAPTER 5 - LEGAL DECISION-MAKING AND PARENTING TIME

Courts may use different words or phrases for what used to be known as "custody". Arizona uses "legal decision-making". The options are Sole Legal Decision-Making, Joint Legal Decision-Making or Joint Legal Decision-Making with one parent having final decision-making power if they cannot make a joint decision. Legal Decision-Making does not control Parenting Time.

Legal Decision-Making

It seems most states now want to have parents share the legal decision-making responsibility for medical decisions and educational decisions. That means that the parents must be in agreement regarding school choice, medical treatment, doctors and the like. It is interesting since many parents cannot agree on anything. It is really important to show, via email or texts, that you are ready, willing and able to co-parent. If your ex disagrees just to disagree, make sure you preserve any evidence showing that. For example, if you are trying to pick the child's school, provide an email where you provide explanations of why you chose the school you chose.

Whether or not you have joint or sole legal decision-making depends on the facts and circumstances in your case. It is typically based on whether or not you and your ex can co-parent together. If you can co-parent together, the court will likely order joint legal decision-making. However, if there has been significant domestic violence, substance abuse, child abuse or your ex was involved in a violent crime the court may not. Check the laws in your state.

Parenting Time

Parenting time is the time that each parent will care for the child(ren). Division of parenting time can range from one parent having 100% of the parenting time to the parties dividing parenting time 50/50 and anything in between, including one parent having only supervised parenting time.

Although most, if not all, courts would prefer parents equally share parenting time, there are several issues that could arise to cause the court to limit a parent's parenting times. The typical issues that arise are child abuse, domestic violence, substance abuse, mental health issues, work schedule and the like.

Custody Evaluations

If you or your ex make an allegation of child abuse, domestic violence, drug/alcohol abuse, the judge may appoint a neutral third party to investigate. In Arizona we have Court Appointed Advisors (CAA), Focused Assessments (FA) and Comprehensive Family Evaluations (CFE). If there are allegations about child abuse, the court may appoint a Best Interest Attorney (BIA).

Court Appointed Advisor

The CAA, who is a lawyer or mental health professional, will investigate any issues the Judge deems necessary. The costs for the CAA are usually divided between the parents. However, sometimes if the parties are indigent, the Court may order that the state or county pick up the tab. The CAA usually just investigates and reports back. There are not necessarily "findings" or "recommendations".

Focused Assessment

The Court may also want to have some kind of assessment or evaluation completed for just one or two issues. In that case, the judge might appoint a mental health professional to do a Focused Assessment (FA) sometimes referred to as a Limited Scope Assessment (LSA) wherein a mental health professional investigates just one or two issues. For instance, if there is an accusation about substance abuse, the mental health professional will only investigate that one issue. The professional who is completing the FA may require one or both parents to submit to random drug test and/or order a hair follicle test. They can also do home visits, interviews with witnesses or collaterals, interview the child(ren) or request someone else interview the child(ren). They have a lot of leeway and their only job is to provide the Court with information that will help the judge make an informed ruling.

Comprehensive Family Evaluation

The judge may also order a Comprehensive Family Evaluation (CFE). A CFE is a full custody evaluation on the family that may include mental health evaluations, substance abuse evaluation, child abuse evaluation, domestic violence evaluation, psychological testing, home visits, interviews, review of documents/medical records/counseling records/school records, and interviews or intake forms from collaterals. This is a very comprehensive evaluation and should not be taken lightly. Upon completion of the evaluation the evaluator will prepare a report for the court. The report will list several recommendations which should include recommendations for legal decision-making, parenting time, counseling and the like. They will also very likely prepare a parenting plan of sorts with recommendations for holiday parenting time, travel notification, first right of refusal, child exchanges and communication between the parties. You should make sure to communicate exactly what you want for parenting time and legal decision-making to the evaluator. Look at sample plans online and review my parenting plan tips below.

In Arizona an average CFE will cost $10,000 - $30,000 dollars to complete. If you want to depose the evaluator or have her testify in court, that will cost extra. I wrote a book to teach you how to prepare for these evaluations. It is called _Custody Evaluation Preparation_. If you are having a custody evaluation done, I cannot state how important it is to get prepared. At minimum you should read my book. However, if you can find someone in your area to prep you for the evaluation, do it. It is so important not to mess this up.

Judges may also interview the children or order that the child(ren) be interviewed by a neutral third party who is trained to interview children. The age of the child will likely be a determining factor as to whether or not the child gets interviewed. If your children are interviewed, they will be asked questions about home life and about each parent. There are things you can do as a parent to prepare for this, such as putting a picture of your ex in your child's room and saying something nice about your ex to your child. My book on custody evaluations goes into this much more in depth.

Best Interest Attorney / Guardian Ad Litem / Child's Attorney

A Best Interest Attorney (BIA) is an attorney who litigates for what is in the best interest of the child. They can present evidence, talk with attorneys and file documents on behalf of the child's best interest.

A Child's Attorney is different than a Best Interest Attorney or even a Guardian Ad Litem. The child's attorney must do what they child wants, whether or not it is in the child's best interest. A best interest attorney must argue for what is in the child's best interest. Guardian ad litem may not even be required to be an attorney in some jurisdictions and they have rules separate and apart from attorneys.

EXAMPLE: If you represent a child who wants to have ice cream for breakfast, lunch and dinner, the best interest attorney would likely decide that ice cream for breakfast, lunch and dinner was not in the child's best interest and would argue and litigate against that. However, child's attorney would have to argue and litigate for having for what the child wanted despite it not being in the child's best interest.

Drug and Alcohol Use and Abuse

Dealing with drug and alcohol abuse allegations has become common place for courts around the country. Some jurisdictions have even created "drug courts". Drug and alcohol abuse is a serious problem and can affect a person's ability to parent. Therefore, their parenting time and legal decision-making may be decreased. Courts typically won't hand over a child to an alcoholic or drug abuser. But the court also might not see it as a huge horrible thing. What the Court will likely do is set up parameters to keep the child safe while still allowing the drug/alcohol using parent to have parenting time. This may be in the form of supervised parenting time or limited parenting time. It will largely depend on the facts of the case and the requests of the other parent.

If you are worried about the other parent abusing drugs or alcohol, try to come up with a plan that would make you comfortable. For instance, should they drug test weekly for 6 months? Should they go to rehab? Should the parenting time be supervised? You want to come up with a reasonable plan so the judge doesn't think you are just trying to eliminate the parent from your child's life. Make sure to relay that information to the court and/or to the evaluator.

Recreational Drugs

If you use recreational drugs, STOP NOW. You will need to assume that there is some evidence somewhere of your drug use - pictures, texts, screenshots of snapchat or twitter messages. Your ex will use those against you.

If your ex uses recreational drugs, get texts, pictures, videos or screen shots for proof. Ask the Court to require your ex to take random drug tests. If allegations are made about your drug use, the court may require you to take a drug test.

People who do not have a drug use history will often submit to testing and ask the court to require the accuser to pay for the drug test when it comes back negative. People who are drug users will usually fight this. However, sometimes non-drug users will object on principal. Therefore, just because someone is objecting does not mean they use drugs.

Medical marijuana

Many people who use marijuana recreationally obtain a medical marijuana card which allows them to legally use marijuana. However, simply because a person has a medical marijuana card does not mean the person is not abusing marijuana. I have seen custody evaluators address medical marijuana abuse. This can be addressed the same way abuse of prescription pain pills would be addressed. Sometimes judges and mental health experts forget about that and don't think there is anything they can do. If that happens, ask them what they would do about someone abusing pain pills?

Whenever I tried to prove someone with a medical marijuana card was abusing marijuana, I would ask them where they purchased their marijuana and I would ask for receipts. If a previous user gets a new medical marijuana card, they often don't stop using their old supplier. So, they are still purchasing their marijuana illegally.

Driving after using marijuana is just as illegal as driving while drunk. Do not drive your child after smoking marijuana - even if you have a marijuana card. If your ex is the one driving the children after using marijuana, try to find evidence of that to give to the court. Often marijuana users do not know how long they should wait to drive after using. If you know that answer and you ask them in court how long they waited to drive, you may be surprised that they do not know the answer. If you do that, make sure you present evidence to the court on how long the marijuana user should wait before driving.

Alcohol Abuse

Alcohol use is legal in the United States. Many people consume larger quantities of alcohol when they are going through a divorce. Although increased alcohol consumption during the divorce process may not be abnormal, abusing alcohol, even if temporary, can cause a judge to limit your parenting time and decision-making power. Likewise, getting charged with driving under the influence can cause a judge to limit your decision-making power and parenting time. If you are incapable of making good decisions for yourself you may not be able to make decisions for a child.

If you are drinking more alcohol than normal, do not do so around your children and definitely do not drive after consuming alcohol. When children are interviewed and there is an allegation about alcohol abuse, expect that your children will be asked if they have ever seen either parent drink or if they have seen either parent drunk or drinking and driving. Make sure your kids know that you are drinking soda or water or tea or coffee, but be discreet about it. Maybe say, "this lemon water is really tart" or "man this coffee is hot". There are so many ways to get your point across without saying - "Hey look, I'm not drinking alcohol".

Prescription drugs

Just like alcohol, marijuana or any other drug, prescription drugs can be abused. Be sure you know your limits when taking prescribed drugs. If it says don't operate heavy machinery while on the medication you probably should not get behind the wheel of a car. If it says to take one per day, only take one per day. If you mysteriously keep spilling them or losing them or going to different doctors to get different kinds of them the court will catch on. Do yourself a favor and get healthy before trying to fight for your child.

If your ex is addicted, you will need to have proof to give to the court. Saying that your ex takes too many pain pills or ADHD pills may not go very far. However, giving specific examples may carry more weight. If your ex is obtaining the drugs legally, there should be a record in the state pharmacy database. However, if your ex is buying on the black market or dark web, then it will be much more difficult to prove.

If your spouse is being drug tested, he should test positive for the prescribed drug he is taking. If that happens, the facility can do further testing on samples that tested "positive" for the drug and see if the results equal the amount prescribed. Check with your testing facility to see they can do this.

Illegal drugs

Given the huge increase in children being born addicted to drugs, it is clear that many parents are addicted to illegal drugs. If you are addicted, please get help now. You will not do your child any good if you cannot control your addiction.

If your ex is addicted to an illegal drug, do what you can to get proof to show the court. Again, emails, texts, records from a rehab, criminal records or pictures help the court determine whether your ex is using illegal drugs. Also ask the court to order your ex to submit to a drug test. The first one should be hair follicle and urine to be sure to get results for the longest period of time.

Drug and Alcohol Testing

There are several types of drug/alcohol tests: Urine, Hair Follicle, Blood and Fingernail. You will also want the court to order that the person get tested in a facility that watches the person urinate so they cannot cheat the test.

When asking for your ex to be randomly drug tested by urine sample, it is important to be specific on how you want the random drug testing to be done and it is important to be specific as to why you believe they are using drugs. Drug tests can be weekly or monthly. But you need to know the pros and cons for each. For instance, if you ask for a random weekly drug test, the test may be done on a Monday or Tuesday so the drug or alcohol user may be able to use immediately after the test on Monday or Tuesday and still come up clean the following week depending on what is being tested. I like to request the court to order six random monthly tests. That way there is usually at least one a week, but there could also be two a week.

You or the court may also request that a hair follicle be tested. You might remember when Britney Spears shaved her entire body, including her head because she was going to be drug tested. If your ex shaves his entire body, you can ask the court to assume he would have tested positive. However, there is also fingernail/toenail testing. So, if you end up in court facing a newly shaved ex, ask the court to test her fingernails/toenails and if they are long enough, and ask the court to order her not to cut them before testing and that the testing be done within 24 hours.

If your ex has dyed or bleached her hair, that may affect the result of the hair follicle drug test

Parenting Plan

A parenting plan is really just that, a plan about how you will parent and co-parent your child. This plan should define regular parenting time, holiday parenting time, birthday parenting time, vacation time, daily care of the child, first right of refusal, and the like. You will need to address where exchanges will happen and who is responsible for transportation. You may also wish to address birthday parties and who is allowed to attend and who will pay. It is a good idea to have these things buttoned down. Even though you and your ex might work really well together now, that is likely to change when a new significant other comes into the picture.

> **EXAMPLE**
>
> I have a client who agreed with her ex that Mother would always get 9am-12pm on Christmas Day because there had been a long-standing Christmas tradition where the family would go to the maternal grandmother's home. They would celebrate with siblings, cousins, nephews and nieces. It was really the only time the family would get together like that. Father agreed that it was a good tradition for the children to maintain. The parenting plan stated that the parties would allow the children to participate in family traditions. The only family tradition at the time was maternal grandmother's Christmas tradition.
>
> Father got remarried. Father decided that he wanted to start his own traditions. He decided that he wanted that tradition to take place at exactly the same time as maternal grandmother's tradition.
>
> It should be known that my client and her ex-husband entered into a consent decree. They agreed on everything - parenting time, division of two businesses, division of property and debt - EVERYTHING. They even agreed on the entire parenting plan. It was not until Mother got remarried that Father decided to stir the pot. Even though Father had been remarried for years and by all accounts was happily married, Mother's remarriage was a trigger for him. I don't think he even knew that it was a trigger, or that he was acting different, but it was.
>
> The parties eventually had to involve a parenting coordinator to help remedy the issue. It was resolved when the parenting coordinator strongly suggested that Father continue to allow the family tradition.

Daily parenting time

Each parenting plan requires some type of daily, weekly, monthly or yearly parenting plan. The plan chosen should be age appropriate. That means that if the child is younger, she should not be away from her primary parent for too long. You can google "age-appropriate parenting plans". For instance, if a mother is breast-feeding a baby, the child maybe shouldn't be away from her for more than a few hours. Below are a few types of parenting plans.

When you are choosing a plan, you need to take into consideration the child's age, child's maturity, special needs of the child, distance between houses, relationship with each parent, work schedules, and even the number of transitions that will take place each week and the stressfulness of each of those transitions.

You will also need to decide if the parenting time will be equal or less than equal. It seems that the courts are leaning towards equal parenting time if all things are equal. Therefore, if you do not want your ex to have equal parenting time, you need to have a really good reason. Good reasons might be significant domestic violence, child abuse, drug or alcohol abuse, and/or a significant personality disorder that interferes with their ability to appropriately parent. If your child has special needs and you are the only parent who has been willing to take the time and effort to care for the child's specific needs, that may also be a good reason. Further, if you are breastfeeding, the court might allow you to have more time. If your ex is just a jerk or had an affair, that is not going to be a reason to keep the child away from him. But, if your ex is putting the child in dangerous situations because of a sex addiction or some other issue, that might be a different story. Just make sure your reasons for not allowing or wanting the child to spend equal time with the other parent are based on real issues that are detrimental to your child and you have real facts with real evidence to back that up.

Equal Parenting Time

Common equal parenting time schedules are 2-2-3, 3-4-4-3, 5-2-2-5 or week on week off.

2-2-3 Schedule – This plan is often used for younger children who don't do well being away from either parent for a significant amount of time. This parenting plan has 3 exchanges every week and allows for parents to have full weekends with the children every other weekend.

The con is that transitions are difficult for young children, so three transitions could be difficult. Another problem is that the children may have a difficult time remembering where they go because there are really no set days. The parent days actually alternate weekly. For instance, week 1 Mother may have the children Monday, Tuesday, Friday, Saturday, Sunday. The next week Mother has the children Wednesday and Thursday. This is not an easy schedule for anyone to keep track of.

Sun	Mon	Tues	Weds	Thurs	Fri	Sat
DAD	MOM	MOM	DAD	DAD	MOM	MOM
MOM	DAD	DAD	MOM	MOM	DAD	DAD
DAD	MOM	MOM	DAD	DAD	MOM	MOM
MOM	DAD	DAD	MOM	MOM	DAD	DAD

    3-4-4-3 Schedule – This plan is also typically used when the children are young and find it difficult to be away from any parent for more than 3-4 days.

    This parenting time only has two exchanges a week. The parents would have 3 standard days and they would alternate one. The days depend on what days you choose. This works well for families where one parent works weekends. However, I have seen people split the weekends. For instance, one person would get Thursday, Friday, Saturday, the other parent would get Sunday, Monday and Tuesday and they would alternate Wednesday.

    The con to this schedule is that neither party gets a full weekend to make plans. Even though it might seem like a great idea at first, especially if one parent wants to take the child to church weekly, parents usually end up back in court trying to fix the schedule if they cannot reach a resolution themselves.

    If you choose to use the 3-4-4-3 schedule, you may want to add some language that permits you both to take weekends periodically. You may be required to give some amount of notice and you may be required to provide make-up time. But being able to take your children away on a weekend trip can help make great memories. You don't want to lose all ability to take your kids to the snow or to the beach or their grandparents on weekends.

Sun	Mon	Tues	Weds	Thurs	Fri	Sat
MOM	MOM	MOM	MOM	DAD	DAD	DAD
MOM	MOM	MOM	DAD	DAD	DAD	DAD
MOM	MOM	MOM	MOM	DAD	DAD	DAD
MOM	MOM	MOM	DAD	DAD	DAD	DAD

TIP #6

It is important to make sure that your parenting plan includes plans for the future. For instance, if one person works weekends and is fine having only weekday parenting time because the child is not in school, the schedule will most certainly become an issue when the child is going to school full time and the parent who has only weekday time becomes frustrated because his parenting days only consists of homework and school. Make a contingency plan. You may also want to consider what happens if your "weekend" work schedule changes and you have weekends off.

TIP #7

If you have a parenting schedule that provides you every Monday as a parenting day, be sure to add language about make up time for the Monday holidays – if your holiday schedule alternates long weekends or Monday holidays. For instance, if Mother has Mondays, you could state, Father must notify Mother at least one week in advance if he intends to take the Monday holiday. If Father does take the Monday holiday, Mother may choose to have either the following Wednesday or Thursday as make-up time.

5-2-2-5 Schedule

This parenting plan is where one parent has two set days every week, such as every Monday and Tuesday, the other parent also has two set days every week, such as every Wednesday and Thursday; then the parents alternate Friday, Saturday and Sunday. One week there will be 3 transitions and the other week will only have 1 transition. This plan may work well if you have school-aged children and can do drop-offs/pick-ups at school to avoid face-to-face contact with the other parent.

Cons with this plan is that there are a lot of transitions every other week and parents may need to work together to ensure homework is completed and the children are prepared for tests. If you and your ex are high conflict co parents, this may not be the best plan because transitions can be difficult, especially for kids whose parents are in high conflict. If parents are in high conflict, exchanges at school can help lessen the conflicts.

NOTE
The parent who is better at helping the kids' study should probably have Wednesdays and Thursdays since most school tests are done on Fridays.

Sun	Mon	Tues	Weds	Thurs	Fri	Sat
DAD	MOM	MOM	DAD	DAD	MOM	MOM
MOM	MOM	MOM	DAD	DAD	DAD	DAD
DAD	MOM	MOM	DAD	DAD	MOM	MOM
MOM	MOM	MOM	DAD	DAD	DAD	DAD

Week On Week Off

This schedule is just as it sounds, the parents alternate weeks of keeping the child(ren). When choosing which days to exchange the child, it might be best if it is not over the weekend or even on a Friday. Think about when you want to take family trips. Many families leave on Friday right after work. If you are waiting to exchange on Friday it may be difficult to leave when you want. You may also want to stay away from Monday exchanges so the transition does not interfere with 3-day holidays. Maybe you want to make the exchange on a Wednesday so each parent has time to help the child with homework during their week but they don't have the whole week. This may also be helpful in the event one parent continuously fails to participate in helping with homework. There are also less exchanges.

The con of this schedule is that the children are away from each parent for seven days which may be a lot for younger children. This schedule should only be followed when the children are older.

Sun	Mon	Tue	Wed	Thurs	Fri	Sat
DAD	DAD	DAD	DAD	DAD	DAD	DAD
MOM	MOM	MOM	MOM	MOM	MOM	MOM
DAD	DAD	DAD	DAD	DAD	DAD	DAD
MOM	MOM	MOM	MOM	MOM	MOM	MOM

Unequal Parenting Time

Although many courts are leaning towards equal parenting time, there are families who have situations where equal parenting time just doesn't work, for whatever reason. If you and your ex are not going to share equal parenting time, there are several parenting plans that are regularly used.

The most common unequal parenting time schedule is when one parent has the children every other weekend and one night or evening a week. The other parent will have the children at all other times. If you and your ex are very high conflict, school pick up and drop offs might be the best solution so you don't need to see each other very frequently. For example, if Mother has parenting time every other weekend and one night a week, she may pick up the child from school on Friday and drop the child off at school on Monday morning. Mother would then pick up the child on Wednesday after school and drop the child off Thursday at school.

If you want to alter that a bit, you could have a Sunday 7:00pm drop off and have your Wednesdays be from after school until 7:00pm. If you are going to come to an agreement, you really can do any schedule you like.

If you are not going to agree and you are going to ask the court to make the decision, you will want to let the judge know exactly what schedule you want and why you believe it is in your child's best interest.

EXAMPLE:

Your honor, I purposefully chose this schedule because my ex lives 75 miles away from the school and it would take her 90 minutes to get our kids to school on time. School starts at 7am. Therefore, the kids will need to be up, eat and shower before 5:30am. Alternatively, I live 3 miles from the school. It takes us about 8 minutes to get there. We don't need to be on the road until 6:45am at the earliest. Also, the kids can take the bus there and back.

You may also want to offer that your ex can have an extra week or two during the summer to make it fairer.

No Set Parenting Time Schedule

Sometimes one or both parents have professions that do not allow for a regularly set parenting time schedule. For example, pilots often have difficulty setting a regular parenting time schedule. One way to address this is to have the pilot provide her schedule as soon as possible, and the parties set up a new schedule each month. If the parties are in high conflict, this can be very difficult. Therefore, and agreement should be drawn up that is very specific, and that addresses all possible issues. Some issues that might arise might be that the pilot takes off all weekends leaving the other parent to have all weekdays and no weekend; or the pilot failing to provide the full schedule and only provides times she wants the other parent to know about.

A possible resolution for the above issues would be to set a tentative schedule and have the pilot parent bid days that match that schedule. If for any reason the pilot cannot get all the days requested, it would be up to her to reach out to see changes. She should provide a copy of her schedule to help the parties try to resolve the issue. In a case like that, it is often helpful to write that any change to that schedule must be agree to by both parents in writing.

You know your children's needs better than any judge. If you can resolve the issues outside of court it will really help your kids.

Drop-offs and Pick-ups

You need to decide who is doing what driving. Typically, the receiving parent picks up the children. But that is not always the case. Sometimes the parent whose time is ending does the drop-off and sometimes parents meet somewhere in the middle. This is a personal preference. However, if your ex is regularly late, you may want to pick up instead of having your ex drop off.

If there is an Order of Protection or Restraining Order, you may need to choose to meet in a public place. Sometimes parents choose to do exchanges at police stations. This is not always the best idea. First, at some police substations, the police may not be physically present. Second, it may be off-putting to the children. Choosing a public place may be better for everyone involved.

You also need to make sure you have alternatives for exchange locations and times. For instance, you could write that the exchanges will be at school, but if there is no school, the exchanges shall be at 9am, at a specific location, unless otherwise agreed to in writing.

Summer parenting time

Summer parenting time may be different from the school year parenting time. For instance, if your children are older and okay with being away from each parent for extended times, you may want to do week on week off or two weeks on two weeks off during the summer. That allows for summer vacations and the schedule helps ensure the vacations won't interfere with the other parent's parenting time. But you may just want to keep the same schedule year-round unless otherwise specifically agreed to times are set out in your agreement. This is a personal choice. Just remember that whatever choice you make, you want to make sure you let the judge know why your specific plan is in the best interest of the children. (This is especially true if you are in trial and you want parenting time one way and your ex wants it a different way.)

Make sure you have appropriate drop off times and locations for the summer. If the exchange is typically at school, you will need to figure out something else when school is not in session. You will also need to decide who will provide transportation.

If you get along with each other and you trust the other parent to be on time, it can be nice to have drop-offs instead of pick-ups. I feel like it is better psychologically for the kids. It may seem as if you are handing the child over and therefore approve of the parenting time as opposed to picking up and "taking" from the other parent. That may give the appearance you do not approve as much. However, if one parent is notoriously late, then you probably don't want to wait for that person to drop off the child. If one parent is late you may also want to add some language about what happens when a parent is consistently late.

If your ex is notoriously late, you may want to have your parenting plan specifically address consequences.

EXAMPLE

If either parent is more than 15 minutes late, excluding provable emergencies such as a car accident or ER visit, three times, the late parent will forfeit 1 hour of parenting time on their next weekend day of parenting time. This will occur every 3rd time the parent is late.

NOTE: It will be important for the parents to keep track of the late days.

Child's Special Needs

What constitutes special needs may depend on your definition. Does your child require extra care of some sort? If so, what is that extra care? If that extra care requires money, who will pay for it? What happens if you determine your child has a learning disability such as dyslexia that requires special tutoring? Who will pay for that?

What if your child is autistic and needs structure or she will have a meltdown? What if one parent is moving every six months and every time that parent moves it takes the child a month to adjust?

Again, you know your child's needs more than I do and more than a judge does. If you ask a judge for something specific, be sure to provide specific facts as to why and what may happen if the judge does not rule the way you want her to.

Doctor Appointments/Emergencies/Elective Procedures

You should have a whole section on medical issues. Typically, if the parents share legal decision-making, either parent can take the child to the doctor when the child is sick, take the child to the dentist for regular check-ups, and take the child to the ER in case of an emergency.

The following are the issues that frequently arise:

- How much notice must I give when I make an appointment?
- Can I take my child without my ex there?
- Can my new significant other attend?
- Can new significant others take the kids to appointments without a parent present?
- Are both parents permitted/required to attend? This can be problematic. What if both parents are required to attend and one parent is unavailable?
- What about elective procedures, such as braces?
    - What if I don't agree to pay, can I still attend the appointments?
- Who pays for the expenses that are not covered or reimbursed by the insurance company?
- What information do I need to provide to my ex after an appointment?
    - What information would you want? Just send a text or emails with the basics. *Billy was at doctor today. He's in the 85th percentile for both height and weight. Doctor thinks he should be saying more works, so we need to be working with him daily. We are supposed to go back in 3 months. Is there any day that you can't make it? I definitely want to go. Do you?*

There are really no right or wrong answers to these questions. But there should be answers to these questions put into your parenting plan. You know your life better than anyone. Maybe one parent doesn't care. Maybe one parent cares a lot. I've seen situations where an ex wants his new wife to take the child to the doctor or dentist. That parent likely has no legal rights (depending on your state laws) but more importantly, how do you feel about it? It could be a real benefit if both parents work full time. Alternatively, that new spouse is not necessarily bound by the parenting plan. So, who will be providing you with the information?

One issue that comes up pretty regularly is when a doctor wants to medicate a child for ADHD and one parent wants the medication and one parent does not want the medication. How will that get resolved? Maybe you agree to ask for a second opinion or a third opinion for a tie breaker if necessary.

What about vaccines? I have seen people who were pro-vaccine get a divorce and then become anti-vaccine. And what vaccines are okay? All vaccines? COVID? HPV? If you can get agreements on all of these things without court intervention, that would be great. However, if you cannot, be sure to add everything you want into the parenting plan and let the judge know why it is important.

Vacation time

Typically, parents are given two weeks of vacation time. That time can either be consecutive or non-consecutive. Deciding whether to have consecutive or non-consecutive should be based on the child's age, relationship with the parents, regular parenting time and previous history of traveling. For instance, a 2-year-old who only sees dad every other weekend during the year likely should not be away from his primary parent for two consecutive weeks. However, if you have a 10-year-old who spends 50/50 time with her parents, being with one parent for two weeks is probably okay. But 10 is still young and will likely need phone calls or facetime with the non-vacationing parent.

You should also decide if you want vacations to occur only during summer; or, if winter, spring and fall vacations are also okay. I have never understood parents who want to prohibit travel during the other parent's time if it does not interfere with regular parenting time, but some people do. You may want to put a paragraph in your agreement that says *neither parent can prohibit the other parent from traveling in or out of state with the child during his or her own parenting time.*

You will also need to determine rules for giving the other parent information. Typically, the courts require parents to provide an itinerary of travel. Where you are going, how you are getting there - with flight times and numbers, where you will be staying - with an address and phone number and when you will be home. If you are driving, you should provide the route that will be taken.

You must also decide if you are allowed to do a "staycation" and what that means? Can you keep your children for two weeks and just stay home with them or do you need to be traveling if it is going to interfere with your ex's parenting time?

Deadlines for proposed vacation time

Typically, you want to have notice of when the other parent is going to on vacation because it may interfere with your parenting time and you don't want to plan a vacation for the same time your ex has planned her vacation. Therefore, you may want to have the following guidelines in your parenting plan:

If either parent intends to take a vacation that will interfere with the other parent's parenting time, the vacationing parent must give notice 60 days in advance of the vacation. If the parents' vacation days interfere with each other, Father shall have priority in ODD numbered years and Mother shall have priority in EVEN numbered years.

That means if Mother scheduled a vacation from July 6, 2019 - July 12, 2019 and Father had scheduled a vacation from July 10, 2019 - July 17, 2019, Father's vacation would stand since he had priority in ODD years and Mother would need to reschedule.

What you don't want to do is preclude each other from taking a long weekend or traveling during your own parenting time. For instance, you have a week on/week off parenting schedule, you may want to be able to travel during that time without being required to obtain the other parent's approval – but you would still be required to give notice.

Traveling in state

If you are traveling with your child within the state you live in, do you want to be required to tell the other parent ahead of time or even at all? For example, if you live in San Diego, California and want to travel to San Francisco, California (508 miles away) should you be required to give the same notice as you would if you were traveling from California to New York? Or what about if you just do a staycation 15 miles from your home? You need to set parameters that you can both live with. For instance, if either parent flies anywhere with the child(ren), they should provide a flight itinerary within 2 days of travel or one day after scheduling, whichever is soonest.

Traveling out of state

Typically, when you travel out of the state during your own parenting time, you do not want to have to get approval from your ex. So, make sure your decree does not require that. You should, however, provide an itinerary to the other parent. The itinerary should include the date and time leaving and returning along with flight numbers and hotel names. If you are driving, you should provide that information as well. If you are staying at a person's home, you should provide that address.

Traveling out of country

Do you want your ex to be required to seek your permission before traveling outside of the country? Remember, if your ex is required to seek permission to travel outside of the country, so are you. It is normal to have that requirement in the decree. However, if both parents regularly travel outside of the country with the kids, maybe you just need to provide an itinerary. I typically add the non-traveling parent must agree in writing and that permission will not be unreasonably withheld. I also state that the parties will consider the United States State Department Travel Advisories when deciding whether or not withholding permission would be reasonable or not. However, that may not be the only reasonable basis to withhold permission. For instance, if your ex just purchased a home in India and stated he was going to take the child there and you would never see him again, even if the USTA states it is okay to travel to India, it might be reasonable for you to withhold permission.

Passports

You must decide who will hold the passports. Sometimes you can have a neutral 3rd party hold the passports. Otherwise, you will need to agree or have a court decide. Some people alternate holding the passports each year. When people have more than one child, one parent will hold one child's passport and one parent will hold the other(s).

Holidays

Holidays are usually divided between the parents separately from the regular parenting plan. Make sure you have written orders for each holiday. You will also want to have a plan for exchange times and locations. You can either alternate holidays or divide them in half. For instance, Thanksgiving might be divided in half if you have one family who typically eats early and one family that typically eats late. However, some families like to travel over Thanksgiving and some Families just like to hang out for the day. Here is where you could have three divisions of one holiday.

Sample #1 - Splitting Thanksgiving

Thanksgiving - Thanksgiving is defined as Thursday at 9am through Friday 9am. The parties agree that it would be in the child's best interest to split Thanksgiving Day. Mother shall have child from 9am until 3pm. Father shall have child from 3pm until Friday at 9am.

Sample #2 - Thanksgiving as a 4-day weekend.

Thanksgiving - Thanksgiving is defined as Wednesday after school or 5pm if there is no school through Monday school drop off. Father to have Thanksgiving in ODD numbered years, Mother to have Thanksgiving in EVEN numbered years.

IMPORTANT NOTE

If your regular parenting time provides for alternating weekends, the Thanksgiving holiday could interfere with a parent's normal parenting time. When the parents alternate weekends and a holiday interferes with a parent's weekend, the other parent would end up with three weekends in a row. Therefore, you may want to make a plan for make-up time or allow the parent who does not have the child to choose the weekend before or the weekend after.

Example:

If Thanksgiving weekend falls on the parent's weekend who does not have Thanksgiving that year, the parent who does not have the child for Thanksgiving shall have the next weekend. That way each parent would have two weekends in a row.

Sample #3

Thanksgiving - The Day

Thanksgiving is defined as Thursday morning from 9am through Friday morning at 9am. Father shall have Thanksgiving ODD years and Mother shall have Thanksgiving EVEN years.

Sample #4

Thanksgiving Holiday – Thursday and Friday

Thanksgiving holiday is defined as Thursday and Friday and will be equally divided. Mother shall have parenting time Thursday from 9am to Friday 9am in even years and Father will have parenting time from Friday 9am to Saturday 9am.

> NOTE
>
> If you are entering into agreements, you can define the holidays any way you want. For example, you could decide the Thanksgiving holiday could be from 5pm the Wednesday before to 9am Friday the day after.
>
> If you are going to ask the court to decide, be very specific about your requests.
>
> One thing that can be difficult is setting up traditions. So, if you and your ex want to be able to have "traditions" you may want to say something like Mom will have every Thanksgiving Thursday from 9am Thursday to 9am Friday and Father will have Thanksgiving at 9am Friday to 9am Saturday.
>
> I have to begrudgingly admit, my best holiday with my kids was when I didn't have to worry about my kids being required to go to their dads as soon as they were done with Thanksgiving or Christmas. Last year I did Thanksgiving on the Friday following Thanksgiving and I did Christmas on the 27th. Both were the best and most relaxing holidays. So don't be afraid to make your own tradition.

The following are typical U.S. holidays, and should be divided as best fits your family traditions:

- Easter
- Three Day Holiday Weekends - Memorial Day, President's Day, MLK Day, Labor Day (you can have these just go with the weekend parenting time - but if one parent regularly has Mondays, they will lose that if it is not their weekend time. Sometimes parents will say if the parent whose

weekend it is takes the Monday that would otherwise belong to the other parent, the parent who is losing the Monday may have the following Wednesday. If the parent who has the weekend but not normally the Monday opts not to take the Monday, the parent who usually has the Monday will not get the Wednesday. The parent who has the weekend, but not the Monday will notify the parent who has Monday at least 7 days in advance if they are choosing to take the Monday and thereby give up the Wednesday.
- 4th of July - Parents should not plan a summer vacation that interferes with the other parent's 4th of July.
- Veteran's Day
- Thanksgiving - See above.
- Christmas Eve
- Christmas - Christmas, like Thanksgiving can be divided many different ways. Some people celebrate Christmas Eve, some people celebrate Christmas.
- Hanukkah (usually the first day)
- Passover (usually the first day)
- New Year's Eve/New Year's Day usually go together as one holiday.

Birthdays - Parents and child's/children's

I usually recommend that the parents let the birthdays just follow regular parenting time. Of course, most of us want to spend our birthdays with our kids, but you can simply celebrate it another time. And of course, most of us want to spend our kids' birthdays with our kids, but again, we can celebrate another day. Transitions can be very difficult on children, adding another one for a birthday can be tough on the child and splitting a day in half can be even tougher.

Splitting birthdays can be even more difficult on school days. If one parent picks up from school and takes the child out for ice cream, then the child is no longer hungry for dinner. I have seen this happen many times. If you get along with your ex well enough, simply ask if you can see the child for breakfast or drop off a present and give her a hug. But if you aren't getting along that well, it's probably better to just celebrate a different time.

Special occasions

There will be special family occasions such as weddings, reunions, funerals, etc. You want to make a plan for these. Such as the parents agree to allow the parents to take the child to family weddings, funerals, reunions and the like. You know your life and your ex better than me, so make sure you consider who your ex is before agreeing to something like this and make sure you are specific if you think your ex might take advantage of this clause.

> ### NOTE
> You may want to put limits on whose weddings, reunions and funeral the children can attend. For instance, can one parent use this clause to attend the wedding of their third cousin who lives in Italy? You may want to limit it to spouses, children, grandparents, siblings, aunt and uncles.

Extra-Curricular Activities

Extra-curricular activities can cause issues for a few different reasons. First, extra-curricular activities may take place on both parent's parenting time. For instance, if you sign your child up for soccer and practices are Tuesdays and Thursdays with games every Saturday, it will likely interfere with your ex's parenting time. If your child is a star athlete, more practices and games might be required to help foster the skill.

Another issue that often arises, is who will pay for the extra-curricular activity and to what extent. If the parents agree a child will play ice hockey, what does that include? Equipment? Travel? Camp? Tournaments? Each one of those things is an extra expense. Hockey in Arizona is much more expensive than hockey in Minnesota. It's important to understand what you are agreeing to. Also, what if a parent can't afford the expense. Must they agree on it?

We often add a clause that says something like this:

> ### EXAMPLE:
> The parents agree that James should be permitted to play ice hockey. The parties will equally split the cost for James to participate on one team. If James is involved in a tournament, the parties will split the costs pursuant to the percentages of income (or 50/50). If one parent cannot pay, the other parent may pay the entire amount and the child will be permitted to participate. Any other camps or private coaching will be paid by the parent who requests the child attend and those extra coaching sessions and camps should only occur during the paying parent's time unless otherwise agreed in writing.

> Both parents are permitted to attend all games and tournaments no matter which parent pays.

What if you believe the other parent with interfere with extracurricular activities but you know you will want your child to participate, you may want to state that one parent is permitted to sign a child up for a fall activity and one parent is permitted to sign a child up for a spring activity, or parent chooses in odd years and the other parent chooses in even years.

Responsibilities during parenting time

Parents often try to tell each other how to raise the child(ren). They may want to control diet, clothing, sports, friends, telephone time, television programs, movies, games, etc. when the kids are in the other parent's home. It is a good idea for parents to put something in writing about parenting issues that are important to each parent. It should be noted, if there is nothing in the parenting plan, each parent can really do what they want as far as day-to-day care.

Typically, each parent gets to decide things like bedtimes, movies, the amount of time they can play video games and the like. If you have concerns about the other parent's ability to appropriately make those types of decisions, you can try to put something in the parenting plan.

> NOTE
>
> Below are some examples and are in no way required or even necessarily recommended. These types of orders are very difficult to enforce and can create extreme conflict.

Movies and Games

Neither parent will allow the children to watch PG13 movies until they are 13. Neither parent will allow the children to watch Rated R movies or play Rated R games until they are 16. Neither parent will allow the children to watch or play games that are rated MA until they are 16.

Tattoos and Piercings

Neither parent will allow the child to get piercings or tattoos without the other parent's written consent.

Cell Phones
    The parents agree that if and when the child is given a cell phone by either parent, the parent who purchased the phone will ensure there are safeguards on the phone that will block inappropriate content. The parents further agree that GPS may not be used when the child is in the non-purchasing parent's care unless agreed upon in writing.

Co-Sleeping with children
    The parents will not allow the child to regularly sleep in the parent's bed and agree it is in the child's best interest to sleep in his/her own bed.

Haircuts/Dye
    Neither parent shall allow the child to dye his/her hair without the other parents written permission until the child is 13 years old or older. Neither parent should allow the child to cut or dye their hair in violation of the child's school policies.

Right of first refusal

    The right of first refusal occurs when one parent is unable to care for the child. That parent is required to ask the other parent to care for the child while they are unable. It is really important to put boundaries on this. For instance, if you have a 17-year-old son and you want to leave him home while you go grocery shopping, it would be ridiculous for you to be required to let your ex baby-sit. On the other hand, if you have a 5-month-old baby and you are going to be gone for 12 hours, it might be nice to have a right of first refusal clause. So, it might be nice to have clauses to address each age and/or time period. However, it might be less invasive to not have this type of clause.

EXAMPLE

0 - 1 year old - If either parent is unable to care for the child for a period of 6 or more hours, excluding work hours, that parent shall give the other parent first right of refusal. However, if either parent is unable to care for the child for 24 hour or more, not matter the reason, the other parent shall be given the first right of refusal.

2 - 6 years old - If either parent is unable to care for the child for a period of 24 hours along with an overnight, that parent shall give the other parent first right of refusal

---

> 7 - 12 years old - If either parent is unable to care for the child for a period of 24 hours, which includes an overnight, that parent shall give the other parent first right of refusal if they are unable to have the child stay with a step-parent, family member, or the child's friend.
>
> 12 – 17 years old – If either parent is unable to care for the child for a period of 24 hours, which includes and overnight, the children can choose where they want to stay.

Communication

Some courts mandate that you address how and when you will communicate with the other parent. For instance, will you communicate via email, text, or phone? Is the other parent required to respond? My typical clause for communication looks something like this:

The parties shall communicate primarily through email for all non-emergent issues. The receiving parent shall respond within 48 hours unless they are unable to do so because they have no internet service (for instance if they are camping). However, once that parent has email service, they shall respond within 24 hours.

For any issue that needs to be addressed sooner than 48 hours the parents will use texts to communicate. Texts shall be responded to within 12 hours unless they are unable to do so because they lack cell phone service. However, they shall respond within 4 hours once they have cell service.

For any issue that requires immediate attention, i.e., a child has been taken to the emergency room, the parents may communicate by text or phone.

If the other parent is abusive in their communications, you can ask the court to order the parents to use ProperComm. ProperComm edits emails and text messages between high conflict parents to eliminate abuse, hostility and anger. ProperComm is free to victims of domestic violence. The website is www.ProperComm.com.

Introducing significant others

There are rarely clauses put in decrees about new significant others, but I have seen them. If you both want to agree that the children will not be introduced to a significant other for at least a year after the divorce or at least 6 months after they have started dating, you may put that in. However, I'm not sure it will carry much weight and it would be difficult to enforce. But if you both agree, then maybe this clause would be useful.

Long-Distance Parenting Plan

Long-distance parenting plans are used when one parent lives too far away from the child to have regular weekly parenting time. It is up to both parents to ensure the child maintains a healthy relationship with both parents. Even if it is your ex who moved, it is important for the health of your children that you help facilitate visitations. If you are the one who is moving, it is imperative that you continue to let your children know they are important to you and that you love them. You also may need to be the parent traveling in order to facilitate your child's extra-curricular activities. Remember, your children did not choose to have their parents' divorce. The parents did. You need to try to keep your children's lives as normal as possible.

When creating the schedule, be realistic. You must consider the time to travel and cost of travel. If one person lives 100 miles away, it might be okay to have weekend parenting time. If one person lives in California and the other in New York, it will be very difficult to have weekend parenting time. Even long weekends could be difficult for a child to travel that far. So, we will discuss close long-distance parenting plans and far long-distance parenting plans.

Judges will often want to give the out-of-town parent significant summer time, winter break time and spring break times. So, if you are making a proposal for settlement, you may want to make sure you allow for significant time when the children are out of school. But you will also need to be sure that you get to see the child during the summer too. Your child may have a difficult time being away from his primary parent for weeks at a time. It might be good to allow yourself time where either you travel to the other city and stay for a few days or pay to have the child fly back home once or twice during the summer. This can get extremely expensive.

<u>Close Long-distance Parenting Plans</u>

This is a distance that allows either a short flight (1-2 hours) or a drive of 1-3 hours. The drive would be too long for a daily commute for the child but short enough for a weekend trip.

For parenting time, you may want to consider three weekends a month, such as first, third and fourth weekends. Also be sure to state that the first weekend is defined as starting with the first Friday in the month. This parent should also get significant parenting time during the summer.

Because the child has been seeing the long-distance parent during the school year, that parent may not need as much time in the summer. Also, try to ensure that the children see the primary parent during the summer too. It is important not to have the kids be away from the primary parent for too long. If they are young, no longer than two weeks and it would be better if it was only one week at a time for younger children.

Far Long-distance Parenting Plans

Children may have a difficult time traveling back and forth long-distances for short periods of time, such as a weekend, when parents live far away from each other. Even three-day weekends may be too difficult. When parents live far from their children, three or more hours away by car or plane, they need to consider the impact the traveling will have on the kids.

Parents typically divide the winter break so both parents get Christmas time. The long-distance parent typically gets all or most of spring break and fall break. Thanksgiving is usually alternated.

Summer can be more difficult if a young child is involved because the child should not be away from his primary caregiver for weeks at a time. Therefore, parents will often have the children go for no longer than two weeks, return home for two weeks, then go for two more weeks when they are young. Year-round schools offer more breaks through the school year and a shorter summer break. That is sometimes helpful because it allows the children to visit the out-of-state parent during their school breaks. One important thing to remember is that the primary parent also needs vacation time with the kids. So be sure to include that in the offer or request.

TIP # 7

Be sure to add language about extra-curricular activities. If your child is going to be gone three weekends a month and/or all of spring break, fall break, winter break and summer break, he may have a problem participating in an activity. If your child is a talented athlete, you may need to add language that states the parents will work around the child's extra-curricular activities.

Payment for Long-distance Parenting Plan

Some of you may be thinking - well she moved so she should be responsible for the expense. Although that does sound fair, life is not fair. Most courts will require both parties to pay at least some of the expense because visitation with the other parent is usually in the best interest of the child. How much each person pays will depend on each person's income and the judge may also take into consideration who moved and why. But be prepared to pay at least some amount.

You will also want to determine how tickets will be purchased and/or how and when the parent who purchased the tickets will be reimbursed. You don't want to purchase tickets and never be reimbursed, but you also don't want the other parent's failure to reimburse you to interfere with your parenting time. You need to figure out a way to make yourself feel comfortable with payment, or lack thereof. You should also add language that addresses any non-payment or a penalty added for late or non-payment.

You may also want to include a maximum ticket price or total price per year. For example, if a parent chooses to wait until the day before to purchase a plane ticket, should the other parent be stuck with the significant increase in price?

Flying Alone

If your child will need to be flying for the long-distance parenting time, you must decide if your child will fly as an unaccompanied minor or if someone must fly with your child. You should also decide at what age the child can fly unaccompanied. You want this as part of the decree because otherwise it might lead to fighting. Remember, flying with your child can be quite expensive.

Be sure to add a clause about how you will address the issue if a child develops anxiety or a medical condition and can no longer fly alone. You do not want an order saying when the child reaches 12 years old, she can fly alone, only to have that child be unwilling or too afraid to fly alone.

It is also important to understand that some parents will use a child's fear or anxiety as an excuse not to permit the visitation. You may want to add a clause to address that type of interference with parenting time.

Things to Consider for Your Children

If you have a long-distance parenting plan, what will you do about your child's extra-curricular activities?

What happens if your child is a really great football or baseball player and he wants to attend summer camp? Will you let him go? Will he not see his out of state parent?

What if your daughter is invited to a volleyball summer camp, will she go? How will the out-of-town parent get parenting time? It is important to discuss these things prior to entering into an agreement.

If you choose a school in between the parents' houses, how will your child foster friendships?

Might it be better to choose a school by one of the parent's homes? Of course, if the parents live close to each other, that would be the best.

Do you want to co-parent or parallel parent?

Co-parenting is for parents who can work together to solve problems. Parents may attend school functions at the same time and generally do not fight in front of the kids.

Parallel parenting is for parents who cannot work together and who have difficulty being in the same room together. These parents do not participate in joint activities, kids have extra-curricular activities during each parent's time. The parents do not attend any appointments together. The parents only communicate in writing and only when necessary.

This also means that parents may miss important events. If you do choose to parallel parent, you should be specific with what events both parents can attend, such as graduations, principal list awards ceremony, school holiday programs, championship games, etc.

CHAPTER 6 – CHILD SUPPORT

What is child support and why is it ordered? Child support is an amount of money paid by one parent to the other in order to help that parent support the children's needs. Each state has its own formula for child support along with the reasons why their formula is the way it is. Check your jurisdiction. Child support is typically intended to cover housing, electricity, food, water, clothing, toiletries, and the like while at the payee's home. Child support does not necessarily cover all costs associated with the child. For example, if the child is in an extracurricular activity, it may not cover that. If the child has medical issues, it does not necessarily cover that[3], if the child needs tutoring it does not cover that and it typically does not cover educational costs.

Think about it this way, the court in your jurisdiction requires everyone in the same financial situation to pay the same amount of child support. That means, if your child is in tutoring, you are paying the same amount as someone whose child is not in tutoring. Therefore, you may need to make up the difference. If your child is in football, you are paying the same amount as a parent whose child is not in football. Those are extra expenses. Even if you pay child support, you may still need to pay a percentage for other things. Obviously, some parents cannot afford to have their children participate in extracurricular activities. At that point you and your ex should make decisions about how you are going to keep the child an activity. (See parenting plan regarding extra-curricular activities above.)

Determining Child Support

All states have their own "guidelines" for child support. The guidelines control how child support is determined, the length of child support and who qualifies for child support. Some states, just use a percentage of income. Some states consider several different factors, such as parenting time, child-care expenses, income, ages of the kids, insurance expenses, and/or any special needs the child may have. Be sure to know the guidelines so that you pay or receive the appropriate amount of child support.

When reading the child support guidelines, be sure to look at language such as "shall", "must" or "may". There are big distinctions between shall/must and may. For instance, if the guidelines say something like; "The Court SHALL include all income from all income sources", the Court is required to include ALL

---

[3] Child support may cover insurance but not unreimbursed medical expenses.

INCOME FROM ALL SOURCES. However, if the guidelines say; "The Court MAY consider all income from all sources when determining income". That is important. In Arizona the Court MAY consider including income from a second job. But the court is not required to consider that income.

Be sure to carefully read the child support guidelines in your state to determine what factors the court will consider when determining child support and what income will be included.

Parenting Time

Most states base child support, at least in part, on the amount of parenting time each parent has. If you are seeking child support, you will want to be careful about agreeing to give the other parent credit for parenting time they are not taking. Conversely, if you are going to be the payor, you want to make sure you get credit for every single minute of parenting time. Make sure to count vacations and holidays. Those extra 10 - 15 days could make a huge difference.

For states that consider parenting time, the more time the payor has the less money he/she will be paying. Conversely, the less parenting time the payor has the more money the payee will be receiving.

Although I never advocate for using parenting time as a tool to increase or decrease child support, it is a factor and you should know what effect the parenting time will have on how much you pay or receive.

Income

Income can sometimes be difficult to determine. Each state will usually provide guidelines as to what money they consider to be "income". It is pretty easy when someone works one job and receives a W-2. It gets a little trickier when one parent is self-employed and writing off personal expenses. The Arizona court requires many of those items to be added back in for determining income, such as cell phone expenses, vehicle expenses and the like. It can also get tricky if the parent has a second job or is working below his or her earning ability.

Although tax returns may be used to determine "income" for tax purposes; taxes do not always accurately reflect a person's real income for child support purposes. If a person is self-employed or receives a K-1, be sure to check the write-offs to see if any of them are not reflective of real expenses or losses. For instance, if a person takes a write off for "depreciation", that expense may be allowed for the IRS but is not a real "expense" as far as determining income. Depreciation of a vehicle or building just means that you are saying the value of that asset has decreased and you are taking that decrease of value as a "loss" for tax purposes. However, in reality, the building still exists and the car still exists and there was no new out of pocket expense for that reduction of value for the asset. Therefore, if you are requesting the other party pay you child support, make sure you add depreciation back into the equation. If there are many write offs, it might be worth it to ask a forensic accountant to help you determine the person's real income.

If you are the person required to pay child support, you probably do not want to pay any more than absolutely necessary. The more money you earn, the more you will pay. If you have legitimate expenses, make sure to write them off. If you own your own business, make sure to count all expenses and be able to explain why those expenses are necessary for running a business. Some states will require you to add some expenses back in. For example, Arizona may require cell phone expenses be added back in. However, if you can explain why that is a legitimate expense, you may not be required to add that back in. For instance, if you only use the phone for business and you have a second, personal phone for which you pay the bill there would be no reason to add it back in. It may be the same for a company vehicle.

Spousal maintenance is usually considered income for child support purposes. The payor of spousal maintenance will deduct if from their income and the receiver of the spousal maintenance will likely be required to add it to his or her income for child support purposes. It is very important to know and understand guidelines for determining the amount of child support in your state.

Age of the children

Some courts will bump up the amount of child support required for older kids. Older kids eat more, have more clothing expenses, driving expenses and the like. When determining your child support, make sure you use the child's accurate age.

Any special needs or expenses of the child.

Some children may need regular tutoring, counseling or medications. Make sure these items are added in as an extraordinary expense, if possible, under your guidelines.

Cost of medical/dental/vision insurance.

Insurance can be tricky if you work for a company that provide insurance that covers you, and your new spouse, your new kids, and the children you have with your ex. Try to find the most reasonable way to break down the costs. For instance, if it costs $50 to insure just you and $250 to insure you and a spouse and $600 to insure you a spouse and all your kids, you may need to subtract $250 from $600 which is $350 and divide that by the number of children you have. Let's say you have 3 kids with your ex and 2 kids with your new spouse. You would divide $350 by 5 which would be $70 and multiply that by the number of children you have with your ex - 2 x $70 or $140 insurance expense for the two kids with the ex. This is just an example and may be done differently in your jurisdiction.

Cost of child-care

Make sure to keep receipts for all payments made to your child-care provider. If you are paying a parent or a friend to babysit in cash, maybe it is time to write a check so you have proof. Simply saying that you pay someone to watch the kids may not work if you don't have receipts.

Child-care expenses usually only include the child-care expenses associated with those expenses necessary to allow you to work. It does not typically include babysitting expenses you incur for when you go out to have fun without the kids. However, there may be a blurry line here. For instance, if you need to go to a marketing event and you need a child-care provider for that time, you should try to include it. There are no guarantees the court will allow it, but it can't hurt to ask. Just make sure you let the court know why it was a necessary expense for business.

Extracurricular activities

Usually, extracurricular are not included in child support. Some states will not even address them in an original decree or parenting plan. Keep that in mind when you are paying for things like field trips or soccer expenses. It is best to have an agreement between both parents in writing. Otherwise, you may not be able to collect.

Other Children from Different Relationships

If you or your ex have a child with someone else, that may also be a factor. Some jurisdictions allow you to include children you are financially responsible for. However, some jurisdictions only allow you to include children that were born prior to the marriage. Therefore, if an affair resulted in the birth of a child, some jurisdictions would not allow that to be deducted. On the other hand, some jurisdictions allow any child to be used as a deduction. Again, know the rules and guidelines in your jurisdiction.

Tax Exemptions/Deductions/Credits

As stated above, I do not give tax advice, so it would be helpful to speak with a CPA or tax expert to determine what, if any benefit you will get from being able to claim your children on your tax returns.

Who gets to claim tax exemptions may be determined by child support guidelines? Check your local statutes and/or child support guidelines to determine who should get the tax benefits. This can also be important when negotiating. If your income is so high that you don't receive much, if any, tax benefit for claiming the kids, maybe use it as leverage with your ex. You can give your ex the tax benefit and get something else in return.

The tax exemptions for the kids may help you negotiate less child support or spousal maintenance.

Don't forget to ask for the child credit. This has been argued quite a bit since COVID.

Age of Majority

Parents are usually obligated to support the children until they are at least 18 years old and have graduated from high school. Some states require parents to support their children when they are older. And, if a child has special needs and is unable to support himself, then the child support may continue well into adulthood.

> ## TIPS
>
> There are some factors in child support that are subject to mistakes and/or arguments. Again, these factors will vary by state - some states may not use any of these factors and some states may use different factors. But this will help you see how you can change facts to help them work for your benefit.
>
> - Working a second job
>   - If you are the payor, you will not want this included as income. Therefore, you may need to prepare arguments as to why that should not be included; such as that the job is temporary or that you are just trying to pay off some bills.
>   - If you are the payee, you will want that included. If your ex regularly worked a second job during the marriage it may count.
> - Child-Care Expenses
>   - If you are paying child-care expenses, be sure to have proof of the expenses. Receipts are helpful to prove costs but a cancelled check might be necessary too if you are paying a family member or friend to care for your children.
>   - If your ex is the person claiming child-care expenses, make sure there is proof. Sometimes parents claim they are paying a family member to care for the children when they are not. Get proof.
> - Insurance Expenses
>   - Make sure to include all insurance expenses, such as medical, dental and vision.
>   - Make sure only the amount for children in common is used in the formula. This can be tricky if a whole new family is added to the insurance. See example above.
> - Spousal Maintenance is usually considered income to the receiver and is deducted from the payor's income when computing child support amount.

Some states have established post-minority child support, meaning some states may require child support be paid after a child reaches the age of majority. Check your state's statutes and guidelines. If you do not want to pay child support after the age of majority, make sure you make a case for it, i.e., the child is not attending school/college and/or the child is capable of working and earning a living, the child does not have mental or physical health problems that would require you to support him or her. On the other hand, if you want to collect support after the age of majority, make sure you provide significant reasons - i.e., the child is in school full time and cannot work or your child has special needs and is unable to be self-sufficient. Make sure you provide evidence of those fact, such as doctor records or records from a caregiver.

NOTE

If you have always worked a second job, the court may be more inclined to consider using that income because it is the status quo. Alternatively, if you are working a second job to pay your lawyer or pay off community debt, then make sure you let the court know that. You may also want the court to know that working the two jobs you are working is not sustainable for a long time or that you are doing only short term because you are now going to be taking care of the kids more often.

NOTE

Most, if not all states have a child support calculator. Basically, you just fill in the blanks.

IMPORTANT NOTE

Your children should not know if you are paying child support or if you are receiving it. Although child support has everything to do with them, it is none of their business.

Payor - Do not tell your children that you are not going to buy something for them because you pay child support and that should be paid for out of child support. Keep your children out of it.

CHAPTER 7 – SPOUSAL MAINTENANCE/ALIMONY

Each state has their own statute with specific factors that a court must consider when determining if any spousal maintenance will be paid and if so the amount of spousal maintenance that will be paid. Some jurisdictions even have calculators to make it easy. Be sure to read the statutes carefully. Some states allow for deviations from the calculator. This might be important, for example, if the calculator has a cap on the amount of income it will consider.

IMPORTANT NOTE

When researching this book, I came across several spousal maintenance calculators.

PROCEED WITH CAUTION.

One website had an alimony calculator for Arizona. Arizona does not have a calculation for alimony. The calculator seems to use an outdated formula. Just be cautious and try to use a calculator from the state or county web-sites in your state, if possible.

Most statutes require the court to consider length of marriage and both parties' incomes. Some also consider the age of the parties, their ability to earn income and the lifestyle to which they are accustomed. Again, know your statute. You will want to provide proof of each factor.

For example: If you were married for 20 years and you were a stay-at-home parent and did not work outside the home, you can bet your ex will want you to find a job. Most courts will not want to require your ex to pay spousal maintenance for an indefinite amount of time. Therefore, you will either need to convince the court you are not able to work, or if you do work you will still need help meeting your reasonable needs, or you will need a plan to begin working so you can get financial help while you are planning.

The plan below is based on Arizona law because Arizona does not have a spousal maintenance calculator. I have actually seen calculators online that are fake. Do not believe all calculators.

You should determine what you would want to do if you are required to go back to work. What is your dream job? Then research what it will take for you to be hired in that position. So, for instance, if you want to be a counselor, what will you need to do? Well, you may need to go to college and possibly even get your master's degree. If you don't have a diploma, you may need to get your GED. How many years will it take? How long will it take to build up your business to a point where you can support your reasonable needs? If you want to own your own bakery shop, you need to provide proof about your qualifications to bake, cost to open a bakery and purchase all the necessary supplies and provide the court with information that would convince them that you could actually run a bakery. So maybe you need to take a business class or get a small business loan. Just have your ducks in a row no matter what you want to do.

Don't just go to court and say I need spousal maintenance. Tell the court how much you need and why you need that much. Don't act like an entitled spoiled princess. Be humble and let the court know that you are doing everything you can. Give the court documents to show them what you have been doing or how you have come up with your plan. If you have applied for jobs, make sure to provide all the information you can. For instance, provide the name of the company, the date and time you applied. If you applied online, print out a copy of your confirmation or take a picture with your phone and print that. If you went to a physical location, make sure you get a name and a business card. It is important to show the court you are trying.

If you would be the payor, and you do NOT want to pay spousal maintenance, here are some tips for you.

1. If there is no court order, don't just give your ex unlimited funds while going through the divorce. Get your ex on a strict budget and be sure that she knows you will not be providing any other financial help. Don't let her charge up all your credit cards either. Maybe leave just one open with a limited value and cancel the rest.

2. Try to get your ex working before you file for divorce.

3. Try to decrease your ex's spending habits prior to filing for divorce. For instance, if you are vacationing in another country three months a year, stop. If you or your spouse are going to spas regularly, stop. Just try to limit the unnecessary expenditures. This will help when it comes to keeping your spouse living in the manner he or she accustomed to.

You may also need to hire a vocational expert to determine the best and quickest path for your ex to become self-sufficient.

Vocational Evaluation

Vocational evaluations are used to determine a party's earning ability and/or to determine how long, if ever, it will take a party to become self-supporting. Evaluations may be used if either party is requesting child support or spousal maintenance and one party believes that the other party is voluntarily either under employed or unemployed. They may also be used if one party has not been in the workforce for several years and is claiming they need support.

Example #1

The parties have been married for 15 years. Both parties have worked the entire 15 years. Husband was earning $250,000 per year for all but the last year and Wife has regularly earned $60,000 per year. The past year, Husband voluntarily quit his job and has taken a job earning $80,000 per year. Most states won't allow Husband to base his earning potential and annual income on that amount because Husband is voluntarily working below his earning capacity. On the other hand, if Husband's job was so stressful that it was causing health issues, then he may be allowed to voluntarily lower his earning capacity.

Example #2

Husband and Wife have been married for 18 years. Wife was a stay-at-home mom, but she has her PhD in computer science which she received over 30 years ago. Husband does not want to pay spousal maintenance, so he hires a vocational expert to determine Wife's earning capacity and to find out what it will take to make Wife's skills current. Wife may want to do her own research in an effort to show none of the skills she learned 30 years ago are useful now.

If you are the spouse being interviewed by a vocational expert, be sure to mention any health issues that could preclude you from working full time or finding a position that would pay enough income not to need spousal maintenance. For instance, if you have mental health issues, back issues, forgetfulness, or if you are unable to stand or sit for long periods of time, be sure to provide that information to the evaluator. You should also provide doctor's notes or medical records. Also, if there is no way you could go back to school because your brain just doesn't work like it once did, let the evaluator know that too. (Keep in mind that any ailment that interferes with your ability to work may also interfere with your ability to care for a child.)

CHAPTER 8 - DIVISION OF ASSETS AND DEBTS

Division of Assets

When people get married, they usually acquire at least some assets during their marriage. They may purchase a car, a house, furniture or stock. They may accumulate property, retirement accounts, jewelry, boats, electronics, guns and the like. They may also have bank accounts that include the income they have earned during the marriage.

Unless you have a prenuptial agreement and/or kept all your property separate, you will need to prove what was earned and acquired before marriage and after marriage. That information will help the court determine what assets need to be divided.

Community Property State

If you live in a community property state assets acquired during the marriage are typically considered both parties' assets and should be divided equally. There are currently only 9 community property states at the time of writing this book. Arizona, California, New Mexico, Louisiana, Texas, Washington, Idaho and Nevada.

In a community property state the parties own everything acquired during the marriage equally, unless there is a prenuptial agreement or one of the parties signs away his rights. Therefore, when the parties divide assets in a divorce, they are typically divided equally. However, for example, since a car cannot be divided equally, the person who will keep the car will likely pay the other party one half of the value of the equity (fair market value minus any debt/loan on the car).

Equitable Distribution Property State

If you live in an equitable distribution property state, assets acquired during the marriage will typically be divided equitable. There are not necessarily hard and fast rules in such a case. The division can be anywhere from ⅓ to ⅔ per person. But usually, courts try to be pretty fair. However, if one person worked two jobs because the other party refused to work, that could make the court give that party a little more.

If you are in an equitable distribution property state, make sure you state why you should have more. What did you bring to the table? Remember, the Court will want to be fair and equitable.

Things to Consider for Division of Property

What property is the best to have at this point in your life?

How will you make ends meet given an equal division of all assets and debt? For instance, should you keep the house so you have a place to live or should you take the retirement that provides monthly payments? That depends, can you afford the house; do you have a job; is there any chance you to could get both assets?

Dividing the Property

It is important to remember that not all property and/or assets are the same. For instance, you may have $100,000 retirement account that was funded pre-taxed, meaning when you remove any funds from that account, the funds may be taxed. There may also be a penalty for removing the funds. You may also have a bank account that has $100,000 in it. Giving one person the retirement account and one person the bank account, therefore, might not be an equitable division.

If you received $100,000 in cash, the cash value is $100,000. If you receive $100,000 in a tax deferred retirement, you would not receive a cash value of $100,000. In fact, not only might you be required to pay taxes on every penny you remove, you may also be required to pay a penalty if you removed the money before a certain age. Furthermore, you may be required to hire a specialist to prepare a Qualified Domestic Relations Order (QDRO) which could cost more than $1,000[4], if there was other money in the retirement account that the other person could receive.

Another common asset that does not have an equal cash value is a home or property. If you compare a home with $100,000 in equity (fair market value minus the mortgage amount unpaid) and a bank account with $100,000, those are not equal. First, it will cost significant money to get the $100,000 out of the house. If you sell it, there will be commissions and closing costs. If you refinance,

---

[4] Check the cost of QDRO in your jurisdiction. Jurisdictions such as California and New York will likely have higher costs than Oklahoma and Nebraska.

you cannot take out all of the equity. Also, depending on the amount of equity and what you intend to do with the home, there may be tax consequences. Make sure you speak with an accountant to make sure you are getting a fair deal.

So be cautious when you are dividing property.

Qualified Domestic Relations Order (QDRO)

A QDRO is an order that divides a retirement account or a pension. This is a special area of law and should only be done by someone who has an extensive background in this area.

If you can have this done before the divorce that could be helpful. In rare instances, if the owner of the retirement or pension and has a spousal survival clause that can become an issue if he remarries and dies before the retirement account is divided. In that instance, the surviving spouse would be the new spouse and the ex-spouse could be out of luck when trying to collect.

TIP

Send the retirement company or pension company a letter stating that you have an interest. That way they are on notice.

Prenuptial Agreement

A prenuptial agreement is a contract the parties enter into before they get married which defines how certain aspects of their property will be handled if there is a divorce. For instance, a prenuptial agreement may address property, debt, income and spousal maintenance. A majority of the states follow the Uniform Premarital Agreement Act (UPAA), or have adopted their own version which is probably very similar to the UPAA.

If you have a prenuptial agreement you will want to talk to an attorney to determine its validity. If it is valid, the prenuptial agreement will control the outcome of the issues it addresses.

There are reasons why a prenuptial agreement could be invalid. Some states provide statutes that specifically discuss how a prenuptial agreement can be invalid. Other states have case law that discusses why or how a prenuptial agreement can be invalid.

NOTE: Custody and child support issues contained in a prenuptial agreement may not be enforceable. If your prenuptial agreement contains language addressing child support, legal decision-making or parenting time, speak with an attorney to determine if it is enforceable.

Prenuptial agreements should have a list of assets for each party. If there is not a list of assets, the agreement may not be enforceable.

Post Nuptial Agreement

As stated above, a post nuptial agreement is a contract that is signed between a married couple.

If either party felt forced to enter into the post nuptial agreement, the agreement may not be valid.

Check with an attorney to determine the validity of the agreement. If the agreement is valid and you go to court and ignore the agreement, the court could find you to be unreasonable and you may be required to pay attorney fees.

Valuing Assets

If you wish to divide property, you may need to obtain an appraisal. Examples of things than may need to be appraised are: houses, guns, coins, property, boats, rvs, antiques and the like.

When having a house appraised it is helpful if you and your ex can agree on an appraiser. Really, if you and your ex can agree on appraisers for any property that needs to be appraised, it would be helpful.

If there is no appraisal, the court may be willing to use the following for estimates of property:
- Homes – Zillow
- Property – Zillow
- Businesses – Business Valuation
  - Alternatively, the court may use book value.
- Cars – Kelly Blue Book (KBB)
- RVs – RV Trader or KBB
- Furniture – Craigslist or eBay
- Antiques – eBay
- Coins – eBay

The court will not want to spend too much time trying to determine if your car is worth $5,000 or $4,500. You want to make this as easy as possible. If you go to court and you have had your house appraised, take the appraisal. If you did not have it appraised, take the Zillow Zestimate. If you have a vehicle, print out the Kelly Blue Book Value. If you still owe money on your car, provide a copy of your outstanding balance. If you can put these values onto a spreadsheet, that is even better.

Try to provide proof of value for everything you want. Even one piece of paper that has a Zestimate for a home value is better than nothing and gives the court something to go by.

Another really good way for the court to value an asset is to order the asset be sold and proceeds equitably divided. If you do not provide an alternative way to value the house, the court may have no choice but to force you to sell the property.

<u>Filing Taxes together</u>

I do not give tax advice and highly recommend you speak with an accountant.

When you are married, you are permitted to file joint income taxes. There may be benefits from filing jointly as a married couple. When you are divorced you cannot file jointly as a married couple. If you want the benefit of filing jointly, you must be married on December 31st.

Many people who are divorcing just want to get it done and over with. However, if it would be final in November or December anyway, you may want to hold off having your decree signed until January.

Nonetheless, if your ex is not working well with you, it may be better just to lose the deductions

Again, you should probably speak with an accountant before filing your taxes and/or deciding on a date to get divorced, if you think it will matter.

Community Property or Jointly Owned Business

Did you or your spouse open a business during the marriage? Parties typically don't plan for divorce while opening a new business. It's just not very romantic. Sometimes a spouse will even sign the business over to their spouse in an effort to gain government assistance. For instance, if the business is 51% or more owned by a woman or a veteran, they may be able to get government business, loans, or grants. Just because you sign something over does not mean you do not still have an interest in the business. Hopefully you did not do that. But if you did, you should probably hire a lawyer who can help you untangle that.

Joint businesses can be tricky during a divorce. For instance, who gets to continue working there? How is it divided? How much is it worth?

Unfortunately, I am not going to be able to answer those questions in this book because there are thousands of different scenarios that could be happening. If you have those issues, you should really seek legal advice from an attorney in your jurisdiction. Even if you just pay for a couple hours for a consultation that might save you thousands or even more.

Value of Business

If you want to know the value of your business there are a couple ways to figure that out.

You could have a business valuation done by a forensic accountant. If you do hire a forensic accountant, make sure they are familiar with your type of business. There are nuances in all businesses and an experienced evaluator can make all the difference. For instance, restaurants take in a lot of cash. So how is that counted? Is it all accounted for or do the owners put cash in their pockets and not claim it? Do doctors and lawyers have "good-will" and can that "good-will" be monetized?

If a similar business has been recently purchased, or if you have recently had an offer to purchase on your business that could also potentially show the value of your business. But it is best not to guess the value and it is really important not to believe your ex if he or she tells you the value.

Alternatively, if no other values are available, the court may take the *cash value* of the business, which is basically the value of the assets minus the debts. However, this does not take into account any good will or future income.

Debt

Community Property States

In community property states, debt is divided equally . . . or equitably. In most cases, any debt incurred during the marriage is a joint debt. Keep that in mind. However, if you are attempting to make the other party responsible for a majority of the debt, you will need to show the court why that debt did not benefit the marriage.

When seeking to divide debt, if one person makes significantly more money than the other party, the debt may be divided in a way that gives more debt to the person earning significantly more money. Sometimes debt may also be divided inequitably if the spouse with less income agrees to take less spousal maintenance. For instance, if one person makes $200,000 per year and the other makes $30,000, the person making $30,000 may want to waive some of the spousal maintenance claim if the other party takes a larger percentage of the debt. It makes sense because if the party earning $30,000 is going to be responsible for half of the debt, that party may need more spousal maintenance to support himself and pay half the debt.

Equitable Distribution Property States

In states with equitable distribution laws, debt will be divided in a way that the judge deems fair and equitable. If you are trying to minimize your part of the debt, you will want to provide proof that the debt that is solely in your ex's name was not incurred for the benefit of the marriage. Conversely, if the debt is in your name, and you want your ex to be at least partially responsible, you should provide proof of how the debt benefitted the marriage.

EXAMPLE

When trying to divide up the debt, you look at credit card statements. You find that your ex has run up thousands of dollars at casinos. Let the court know why you should not be responsible for your ex's gambling debt. To show that, you may want to provide proof that you did not agree to your ex gambling. For instance, you may want to show a text or email where your ex said he would be out of town for work on the day there are charges at a casino and hotel nearby. If you have texts or emails where you state that you do not agree to him gambling, that is something you would want to show the court.

When dividing debt in any state, judges want to be fair and equitable. The divisions do not necessarily need to be equal if it would be unfair for one or the other.

TIP #8

When dividing debt, be careful that your ex is not planning to take extra debt in order to lower spousal maintenance or be granted extra assets, and then file for bankruptcy. This can be very problematic. If you waive your right to spousal maintenance because your ex has agreed to take all $80,000 worth of debt, then your ex refuses to pay any of it and files for bankruptcy, you may still be liable and out of luck for your spousal maintenance.

You can maybe add a clause in the decree that you are only waiving or lowering spousal maintenance based on the fact that your ex was taking on all the debt.

Also add a clause stating your ex is liable for whatever you agreed to and that if your ex fails to pay it, he/she must hold you harmless and reimburse you for any amounts you pay and reimburse you any attorney fees paid in trying to collect.

CHAPTER 9 - MISCELLANEOUS ISSUES

Grandparent/Third Party Rights

Sometimes in a family law action, there are persons other than the parents who should be involved in the children's lives or who believe they should be involved in the child's life. Each state's rules are very different when addressing this issue. This is one area where I found little consistency when comparing different states' statutes. However, one common theme that I found consistent across states is that it appears states want to uphold the parents' rights to parent their children if at all possible.

If you believe you are entitled to 3rd party rights, you should review the statutes in your jurisdiction and probably speak with an attorney. New cases are coming out frequently that can shape a third party's right to parenting. You should also try to maintain your relationship with the child. This may be difficult once you file for 3rd party rights. If you determine that you may qualify for 3rd party rights, you should continue reading this book to help you prepare for your case.

Third parties may be granted full custody in some cases or they may be granted visitation; it will simply depend on the best interest and safety of the child, along with your relationship with the child.

If you are a parent and do not want to allow any other person to have third party rights, you should hire a lawyer in your area to see if there are steps you can take to ensure the court will not award the third party any visitation or custody rights. For instance, if you, as a parent, permit some visitation with the third party, the court may believe that is sufficient. Alternatively, if there is a good reason for you not to permit visitation, be sure to provide evidence to the court. For instance, if you allowed visitation and your child comes back saying that grandma says you are a horrible person, you may need to end visitation. I would recommend journaling what happened.

Marital Waste

Marital waste is when one party spends money inappropriately or irresponsibly for their own benefit and not in furtherance of a marriage. Examples would be gambling, drugs, prostitutes, traveling with a girlfriend or buying her jewelry, giving money to family members (this may depend on who and for what reason), selling property below market value (this may depend on who it was sold to and for what reason).

Although waste claims are difficult to win, it is possible if you have the right evidence. For instance, if your ex took out significant money to gamble you may have a waste claim. Make sure you have real evidence. It is your burden to prove. You can't just say, well, he made $100,000 a year and we have nothing to show for it. You need to have real proof of irresponsible and inappropriate spending. Proof would look like bank or credit card statements showing withdrawals of large sums of cash or many withdrawals that equal large sums. But you will also need to determine how much can be considered spending money on a hobby vs waste. Some people spend tens of thousands of dollars golfing around the world. If it is okay to spend $20,000 per year golfing, why would it not be okay to spend $20,000 per year gambling.

By proving marital waste, you may be able to have the Court designate more debt to the other party or more of the assets to you to make up for the inequity of the waste. But if you prove $20,000 in waste, don't expect to receive all of that. You may expect to receive more like $10,000 which would have been your share of the money.

Attorney Fees and Costs

Just because you do not have an attorney does not mean you may not be responsible for paying for your ex's attorney. Although each state has different statutes and rules regarding attorney fees, I think there is a common theme for courts ordering attorney fees. If one party is being unreasonable, that party may be ordered to pay the other party's attorney fees. If one party earns significantly more than the other party, that too could cause the court to order fees.

<u>Unreasonable Behavior</u>

If one party causes the other party to incur more fees unreasonably, that is when a court might order fees. This is especially true when a party does not want to follow the law. For instance, if the law says bank accounts are to be equally divided and one party empties out all the bank accounts, which then requires the other party to get an attorney to get her money back, the court might award attorney fees.

EXAMPLE

The law requires parties to equally divide all bank accounts. However, Wife decides to take all the money from every bank account she can before she files for divorce. Husband hires a lawyer to try to get the money back.

> The lawyer provides Wife with the relevant laws, rules and statutes and asks her to provide Husband one half of the funds she took. Wife refuses to give Husband any money. Husband incurs attorney fees filing motions with the court and even having a hearing. Wife may be required to pay Husband's attorney fees.
>
> However, if during the hearing the court finds out that Husband is employed and earning substantial amounts of money and Wife is unemployed and has no money to her name other than what she took, the Court may not make her pay.
>
> There are always two sides to every story and the court will want to hear all relevant evidence prior to making a ruling.

Income and Funds Available

The court wants both parties to be on the same playing field and have similar resources when it comes to litigating their cases. Therefore, a court may order one party to pay the other parties' fees if she earns significantly more than her ex and/or has significant funds available. The idea is that the court does not want, for example, only one party to be able to hire experts when it might be necessary for both parties to hire experts. The court won't want one party's attorney causing the other party to incur a lot of expenses by making more out of the litigation than it is worth. I have heard litigants say: "I'd rather give the lawyer all the money than give him a penny." Well, if a party is unreasonable, the court may order her to pay all costs and fees.

If the only information you have is that Wife earns $350,000 per year and Husband earns $70,000 per year you might think Wife should be paying Husband's attorney fees. However, if Husband only earns $70,000 because he is very wealthy and inherited a huge amount of money, then Wife likely wouldn't be paying his fees. However, if Husband stayed home with the kids and does not have a large amount of money, and Wife is a full-time dentist, Wife may be required to pay fees.

Facts are very important in all aspects of litigation. It is important for you to present relevant facts to the court to obtain the outcome you want.

Abiding Trial

If either party asks for fees prior to the day of trial, the court may or may not hold a hearing and award fees. It seems some judges just don't understand how difficult it is for litigants to come up with money to pay an attorney. A judge might even have a hearing and state that the "fees will abide trail". That means the judge will make the ruling at the same time he makes the rulings on everything else.

Affidavit of Fees

In order for the court to determine how much money to award one of the parties, the Court will ask for an affidavit of fees. In Arizona it is called a China Doll Affidavit. The court will want to see the amount the attorney charges per hour along with a list of all services performed and the costs associated therewith. The court will likely give a deadline for that affidavit to be filed. The other party will usually be permitted to review the affidavit and file a response. Parties or their attorneys will often review the affidavit and say some services are unreasonable or should not be paid in an effort to minimize the amount they will be required to pay.

CHAPTER 10 - BUILDING A CASE

Discovery

Discovery is the means by which information is gathered during litigation. In most cases your case must be active, i.e., filed with the court before you can send discovery requests to the opposing party, unless your parenting plan or decree permits discovery or requires exhibit exchanges prior to any documents being filed. When there is an active case, however, both sides are permitted to do discovery. You ask for discovery by requesting the other party provide certain documents or provide answers to certain questions. You may also find information yourself through research, or you may subpoena documents, recordings or pictures from a person or business. This is not an opportunity for a fishing expedition and you are not permitted to request information just to harass the other party. If you are feeling harassed by the requests, check your jurisdiction to see how to request a protective order from harassing discovery requests. The information requested should be reasonably likely to lead to admissible evidence. That means that you can request bank account statements if it is reasonably likely to provide you information that you can use in court. Even if the document itself won't be used in court. The information you request just needs to have the likelihood that some usable information will be discovered.

The rules of discovery are typically controlled in the *Rules of the Court* for the jurisdiction you are in. Most courts have rules posted online; the rules may also be stated by the court in a minute entry, order, or self-help packet. There are usually deadlines for discovery. You should review the rules as soon as you start your divorce and write down the due dates on a calendar. If you miss the deadline, you may lose your opportunity to request documents, take someone's deposition, and/or send interrogatories. There may also be requirements to have the other party served which can take time and cause you to go past the deadline.

There are several ways to obtain information through the discovery process.

NOTE

If the rules say discovery must be completed at least 30 days before trial. You will need to count backwards to determine when you need to send out requests, because the other party will have a certain number of days in which to respond. For example, in Arizona, someone usually is allowed 40 days to answer interrogatories from the date they are served the interrogatories (there

> are exceptions). If you want to have all your discovery done by the 30-day cut-off, you will need to add in the 40 days the person gets to respond, so at a minimum you would want to send them out more than 70 days prior to your trial.

Interrogatories

Interrogatories are a written form of discovery request that permits the person seeking discovery to receive answers to questions from the opposing party, without the need for a deposition. Interrogatories must be served upon the answering party. When the opposing party answers the interrogatory questions, they will usually be required to be answered under oath, just as if the person was answering the questions in court. There are two types of interrogatories; uniform interrogatories and non-uniform interrogatories[5]. You may be required to "serve" the interrogatories to your ex, so make sure to review the requirements for your jurisdiction.

Also be sure to review the rules in your area to determine the number of questions you are permitted to ask.

Uniform Interrogatories

Uniform Interrogatories are questions the court has come up with. They may be found in the court rules or in forms provided by your court. The questions are usually pretty basic, but they will provide you with really useful information for your case. For instance, they will address issues such as education, employment and employment history, salary, totals for all income, retirement accounts, bank accounts, and parenting issues.

Non-Uniform Interrogatories

Non-uniform Interrogatories are specific questions you can write for the opposing party to answer. The party is required to answer under oath, just as he or she is required to answer for uniform interrogatories.

You may be limited to the number of questions you are permitted to ask. Be sure to check the local rules in your area.

---

[5] The names "uniform interrogatories" and "non-uniform" may be different in your jurisdiction. Just know that most jurisdictions have two types of interrogatories. One type that is from a form the court may provide and another type is one where someone can created specific and unique questions that pertain specifically to their case.

Depositions

A deposition is an oral examination of a party or non-party witnesses. The examination takes place in front of a court reporter and is sometimes video recorded. A deposition is used to obtain sworn testimony, outside of court, from either a party or a witness involved in your case. Deposition may be recorded by a court reported only or a video recording of the deposition may be requested. If you do request a video deposition, you may be required to specifically state that in your *notice of deposition*[6]. In most jurisdictions, it is uncommon to have a deposition video recorded because it is more expensive. However, video recording a deposition can be helpful to show problematic behavior. It may also help to paint a more accurate picture of what took place during the deposition. For instance, if someone is yelling in a deposition, there is no way to show that if the deposition was not video recorded because the parties only receive a transcript.

Whether you are the person requesting the deposition or you will be the person deposed, i.e., the deponent, it is really important for you to know the rules of deposition. Maybe even have a copy of them printed out. I can personally attest to the fact that many lawyers violate the deposition rules. If you have the rules in front of you, you may be more apt to call someone out on the violations. Knowing the rules gives you power during a deposition. For example, how much is a lawyer permitted to participate in the deponent's deposition. Not much. You should know what their limits and requirements are. Is the opposing attorney suggesting answers? That is not permitted. If the opposing attorney is objecting in such a way that causes the deponent to answer a certain way, that could also be a problem.

If you are the person requesting the deposition, you will be required to set up the deposition and you will be required to hire and pay a court reporter. The court reporter costs vary by location.

Deposition Expenses

Depositions can be quite costly. You will need a court reporter who will charge by the hour. If you wish to have a transcript of the deposition, that will be another fee. If you need the transcript of the deposition quickly, that will substantially increase the cost.

---

[6] If you appear at your deposition to find you are going to be video recorded, you may want to check your rules. If you did not receive appropriate notice, you may be permitted to cancel your deposition.

If you depose an expert witness, you will likely be required to pay for that witness's preparation time (reviewing files and reports), travel time, and deposition time.

Finally, if you do not have an office or conference room to take the deposition, you can usually rent one, which would result in more costs.

How do you make someone appear for a deposition?

Each jurisdiction has rules about how to provide or *serve* someone with a *notice of deposition* and possibly a subpoena requiring that person to appear. You will need to check your local rules to determine exactly what is required. However, most jurisdictions require you to provide the deponent with notice of a date, time and location for the deposition. You must also provide them with enough time to make appropriate arrangements. Check your local rules for time requirements. It is helpful if you work with the deponent or her attorney to set up a time and place that works for all participants.

If you are deposing someone other than the opposing party, you are required to provide the opposing party with a copy of the Notice of Deposition. It is important for both parties to have the opportunity to attend all depositions.

NOTE
It is a common courtesy for attorneys to try to work together to find a date that works for all people involved. However, if both parties are self-represented, and you don't get along well, you may just want to serve your ex with a notice of deposition unless you are required to do something else by the rules of your court.

Who can you depose?

Each jurisdiction has its own rules on who may be deposed. However, in most jurisdictions, *parties* are usually required to attend depositions if they have been appropriately served a *Notice to Appear for Deposition or a Subpoena to Appear*.

You are typically permitted to depose an *expert witness* who will be testifying at trial. Examples of expert witnesses are custody evaluators who have prepared reports for the court, forensic accountants, and vocational experts. You may want to depose them to determine exactly what they will say in court. When asking certain questions or providing new information to the expert during the deposition which they did not consider, you may be able to get the expert to change his testimony.

It is important to know that experts usually charge a significant hourly rate for the time they spend being deposed, travel to and from and preparation for the deposition. It can be quite costly to depose an expert.

NOTE

I usually ask experts to tell me about the weaknesses of their case. For instance, if a custody evaluator determines someone has a personality disorder it may interfere with her ability to parent or co-parent appropriately. You may wish to ask what other information could help the evaluator make a different finding.

If you want to depose a *fact witness*, you may need the permission of the opposing party and/or the court. A fact witness is someone who saw or heard something and intends to testify about that in court. A fact witness may be a nanny, a teacher, or just some stranger that witnessed an event.

How long can someone be deposed?

Again, each jurisdiction has its own rules about the amount of time allowed for deposing witnesses. Be sure to check your local rules because you may need to request extra time through the court. If you are permitted to depose someone for 4 hours, you are not required to use the entire 4 hours. Furthermore, if you need more than 4 hours, you will likely be permitted to go beyond 4 hours if you have a valid reason. A valid reason might be that you are deposing your ex about several different issues, such as a business and bank accounts and retirement and properties and parenting time and child support and spousal maintenance. If you want to depose someone for longer than the time permitted, you should seek the deponent's agreement or obtain a court order before the deposition if possible. Otherwise, you may be required to take the deposition on another day.

Can I object to questions?

You can typically only object to questions for *form* and *foundation*. And even if you object, you are still required to answer the question unless you are advised not to answer by a lawyer, or you decide not to answer on your own[7].

---

[7] If you choose not to answer, the person deposing you may try to get the court on the phone to force you to answer. If they do not get the court on the phone, they may ask the

You can object to the form of the question if the question is not appropriately worded. Examples of a reason to object based on form would be if you were asked a compound question – in other words two questions at a time.

Example of compound question: Isn't it true that you have a girlfriend and you spent money on her regularly.

There are several things going on with this question:
- Isn't it true that you have a girlfriend?
- Isn't it true that you spent money on her?
- Isn't it true that you spent money on her *regularly*?

You may want to answer part of that question yes and part of the question no. For instance, you may have a girlfriend but never spent money on her. You may have a girlfriend and you may have spent money on her once or twice, but not regularly. You may not even know what "regularly" means. Does that mean once a week? Twice a week? Daily?

Therefore, you would say, "Objection. Form". Then, you can either answer the question in a way that provides the answer that you want to give or you can ask the person deposing you to please reword the question. It's best to ask them to reword for clarity.

You may also be asked other types of subjective questions. In that case, just ask for rewording or clarification.

You may also object to a question based on foundation. That means that the question is vague and/or you need more information to be sure to answer the question correctly.

Example: Isn't it true that you smoked marijuana?

The problem with this question is you don't know what time period this question covers. You will still need to answer the question or you can ask for a time period or ask for clarification.

You are still required to answer the question even after an objection, the objection merely preserves the record. That means, if the deposition is used in

---

court to make a negative inference regarding information you refused to provide. Such as, if you refuse to answer a question about receiving a bonus, they may ask the court to assume your bonus is bigger than the bonuses received in previous years.

court, your objection is preserved. However, you may need to take further action during the trial to ensure your objection is noted.

What questions am I not required to answer in a deposition?

You should not answer questions that ask for attorney client privileged information unless specifically ordered to do so by the court. An example of that would be if you were asked: "What did your attorney tell you to do?"

You should not answer questions if you have been advised not to answer by an attorney. An example of that might be any question about a crime you may have committed. In family law that happens regularly with domestic violence, child abuse, tax evasion, theft and the like. It is important for you to know that anything you say in a deposition may be able to be used against you in another case. If you admit to committing a crime in a deposition, that testimony may be able to be used by a prosecutor to prosecute you in a criminal case.

What questions can I ask during a deposition if I am deposing my ex?

You are typically permitted to ask any questions that are reasonably likely to lead to admissible evidence. However, you are not permitted to harass the deponent. In most cases, if you do harass your deponent, she may be permitted to end the deposition. However, there may be specific rules about ending a deposition, such as filing something with the court immediately after ending it. This is another reason why it is important to know the rules before attending a deposition.

How do I get the deponent to testify about a specific document?

If you want to discuss documents with the deponent during the deposition, you will need to provide 3 sets of documents. When you wish to discuss a certain document, you will hand a copy of the document to the court reporter and ask that the document be marked as an exhibit. You will also hand a copy of the exhibit to the opposing counsel (if represented), and you will want to keep a copy for yourself. You will want to be sure to mark your copy with the same exhibit number as the court reporter marked the exhibit. That way you can correctly refer to the document by exhibit number. The court reporter will attach the exhibits to the deposition transcript.

How can I make the deponent answer a question?

This depends on the question. You cannot force a deponent to incriminate himself. Therefore, if you ask a question about a crime the deponent committed, he can plead the fifth and refuse to answer the question. If you ask the deponent about something that is attorney client privileged, he may state there is a privilege and avoid answering the question.

However, if you are asking the deponent about something like bank accounts or spousal maintenance factors, and she refuses to answer, you can typically call the judge[8] and request the judge make her answer. I always have the judges phone number on hand so I can call during deposition. You will need to be sure you have a valid reason for wanting an answer. You may have a mini oral argument with your ex about the requirement for the deponent to answer, so be prepared with the judge on the phone. You will need to provide reasons for why you want the information.

What happens after the deposition is completed?

When the deposition is completed, the deponent will be asked if he wants to read and sign the transcript of the deposition. That means the deponent will go into the office of the court reporter and review the transcript to be sure that the transcript accurately reflects what was said. I always recommend this because I have seen some deposition transcripts that were very inaccurate. If your transcript is inaccurate and the court reporter does not agree, you may be able to ask for a recording of the deposition. Usually, all court reporters have a recording of the deposition on their computer. I have had to seek intervention from a court reporter's boss.

The court reporter should also ask both parties or their lawyers if they wish to purchase a copy of the deposition. You can usually purchase a hard copy or an electronic copy. You will need to purchase it if you want to use it in court. It typically takes about 10 days or so to receive a copy of the transcript. If you need one before the 10 days you may need to request a rush copy which will cost quite a bit more.

How can I avoid being deposed?

Most jurisdictions provide some form of protective order to stop abusive or overreaching discovery requests. Check your local rules to see if you can

---

[88] Check your jurisdiction to see if this is permitted. Some jurisdictions have judges on call. Some jurisdictions simply have you call the judge who is assigned to your case.

request protection from a deposition. You may be permitted to file a Motion for Protective Order. You will need to have a valid reason to ask the court to deny your ex's right to depose you. If you have an Order of Protection against your ex, that might be a good reason to ask to limit the deposition or to permit you to appear telephonically or by video. Motions for protective orders are different in each jurisdiction so be sure to check your local rules. Also, be sure to add specific facts to your motion. Don't simply say that you have an order of protection or that you are a victim of domestic violence. Say something like: "The last time I saw my ex, he held me captive in our home for 2 days and would not let me leave. When I finally tried to leave, he pulled a gun on me". Paint the picture of why you are in fear or why you do not want to attend the deposition.

More likely than not, you will not be able to get out of a deposition. However, you may be able to appear via video or end a deposition early or limit the questions of your deposition if your ex is using a deposition to harass you or find out about information that is not relevant to your divorce. What a court deems "relevant" information varies from state to state. For instance, if you are getting a divorce in a no-fault state, evidence of an affair may be irrelevant. However, just because you believe evidence of an affair is irrelevant, does not mean it is. Evidence of an affair can be used to show that one spouse committed marital waste by using marital funds on a paramour. Evidence of bringing home a different man every night when the kids are home may show a lack of judgment. So just because you think a subject is irrelevant or harassing does not mean it is.

If you have an emergency, be sure to reach out to the deposing attorney or party immediately. An emergency may be a car accident, you are ill or experiencing COVID symptoms, you are in the hospital, or a close family member is in the hospital or died.

How can I best prepare for being deposed?

Preparing for a deposition is important. There are books available or you can hire someone to help you prepare. You may even want to watch a YouTube video or two. Some important things to remember are listed below:

1. The day before your deposition
   - Make sure you have appropriate child-care
   - Lay out your clothes the day before
   - Get a good night's sleep
   - Review any documents they have filed so you can anticipate what types of questions you will be asked.
   - Make sure you get online directions.

2. Before you leave:
   - Put lavender on your temples.
   - Eat a good breakfast
   - If you have time to exercise, try to do so.
   - Leave early. Being late causes stress.
3. You will be given some instructions, such as:
   - Do not say mhm or uh-hu, you need to answer audibly so the court reporter can take down your answers.
   - You may be asked if you are on any drugs that would preclude you from answering honestly.
4. If you are representing yourself during a deposition, you may wish to object on the basis of form and foundation (discussed above).
5. Listen to the question and only answer the question.
   - If you are asked a yes or no question, answer yes or no.
6. Take breaks if you need to take breaks. If you are feeling bullied, take a break. You should answer any outstanding questions first.
7. If you are shown an exhibit, review the exhibit and do not take the word of the person deposing you.
8. The deposing party may speak with you like you are his friend. You are not. Do not get lulled into a false sense of security.
9. Do not try to outsmart the person deposing you.
10. Do not be afraid of silence. It is a common tactic to stare at a deponent and wait for them to say more. If you are done answering the question, sit quietly.
11. Do not get snotty.
12. Do not be facetious. Answer the question appropriately. Answering in a joking way does not look good on transcript. In fact, your answer may be the exact opposite of what you meant.

Can I walk out of a deposition if I feel like I'm being harassed?

Some jurisdictions will permit you to leave a deposition if it you are truly being harassed. If your jurisdiction permits a walk-out, it would be wise to tell the person conducting the deposition that you are feeling harassed and that you do not believe you should be required to answer the questions. In some cases, the person deposing you may try to contact the court. If that happens, be prepared to tell the court why you believe you should not be required to answer that question.

If you do stop deposition after it starts or walk out of the deposition, you may be required to timely file a motion or notice with the court to let the court know that you walked out of the deposition and why you walked out of the deposition. The court may or may not require you to appear at a second deposition and the court may or may not limit the areas or topics that are permitted to be covered.

What may be irrelevant or harassing, for example, may be however, is that if you are 45 years old and were married when you were 30, and are asked if you had an abortion at 16 years old. The abortion should be irrelevant and is being asked for the purpose of harassing you.

How do I use a deposition in court?

Although each jurisdiction has different rules for using depositions in court, each court should permit the use of a deposition if you follow the rules. If you do not follow the rules, you may not be able to have the deposition admitted as evidence.

For example, you may be required to have a sealed deposition transcript that you provide to the court to ensure authenticity. You should be able to receive a sealed transcript from the court reporter. Courts may also require you to designate portions of the deposition that you want to have read or used in court.

EXAMPLE: Page 6; Line 25 – Page 7; Line 10.

You can also write the words associated with those page numbers and lines to ensure the court has access to them. Be sure to read the rules for designation. You may be required to provide them weeks before the trial. You may be required to disclose them sooner rather than later. Each jurisdiction has specific timelines for these types of things.

<u>Subpoenas</u>

A subpoena is a document which commands a person to appear and/or provide documents at or by a specific date and time. Subpoenas are often used to obtain documents that might be important for your case. Even when your ex personally provides documents to you, you may want to subpoena documents to ensure you have received a complete copy of ALL relevant documents. The documents received can be used as exhibits in court, if relevant, or for investigation purposes.

> **EXAMPLE**
>
> Sometimes parties subpoena extensive amounts of bank documents in an attempt to prove the other party was hiding or wasting money. This may enable them to follow where money was spent or hidden. You can do that by comparing paychecks with deposits. Sometimes paychecks are split into two or more bank accounts. For instance, if your ex received a bonus, she may have put it into a different account. If your ex received a raise, she may be putting the increase into another account. She also may be taking money from one account and putting it into another account.

Subpoenas can be used to command or order someone to appear for a deposition or a trial. However, subpoenas can also be used to require a company to appear at your office and bring documents. You can state on the subpoena that if the person provides documents before such date, they do not need to appear in person. This is common for getting documents from businesses. You may be able to obtain a form subpoena from the self-help center in your area.

Subpoenas typically need to served to the party being subpoenaed as required by your local rules. However, some people may accept service of subpoenas by mail or email or fax. Therefore, if you would like to save money, you should ask the witness or custodian of records if they will accept service.

If you want a witness to appear in court, you should definitely provide them with a subpoena. Hostile witnesses may agree to be served by email or mail but fail to appear. In that case, you would need to prove you served them in strict compliance with your judicial rules. The court might accept service by email if the witness said they would accept alternative service, but it is probably better to just spend the money and have them legally served.

The subpoena itself has several requirements to make it valid. Each jurisdiction has their own requirements. Be sure to read all the requirements prior to sending out subpoenas. At minimum they should be on a pleading type document which provides the case names, court, case number, the name of the person being subpoenaed, the location and time to appear and a list of what documents to bring if any. The document should also provide notice for the requirements of the subpoenaed person, along with instructions on how to object to the subpoena. Your rules may also require that the witness receive a check or payment for mileage or other costs, so again, be sure to check your rules. You will also want to check your rules on the requirement to provide a copy of the subpoena to the opposing party or lawyer.

If you are trying to get doctor's records/counseling records for your ex you will need to have your ex sign a HIPAA release. The release will need to be fairly narrowed to ensure you only get the information needed. For instance, if you are trying to prove your ex has a mental health issue, you should probably only request documents associated with mental health issues. If your ex refuses to sign a HIPAA release, you may be able to get a court order for release. Otherwise, you may ask the court to make a negative inference about the party's health.

Out of State Subpoenas

If you are trying to serve a company out of state, you will be required to follow the rules of that state. Each state has different requirements. You may need to seek assistance from an attorney in the other state. However, many businesses, such as banks, will honor a subpoena from another state. You can reach out to the business and see what their requirements are.

Out of Country Subpoenas or Indian Reservation Subpoenas

These are not easy to serve and you will likely need an attorney to help you. Each country and reservation have its own rules.

Can I stop my ex from subpoenaing the company I work for?

It depends. If your ex is subpoenaing the company you work for just to harass you, then you may be able to file for a protective order. However, there may be a lot of relevant information your ex may be permitted to receive from that company. For instance, your ex has the right to see your salary history, any benefits or perks, possibly your personnel file and any contracts your might have with the company. And even if you have provided all that information, your ex may want to have the information provided directly from the source to ensure authenticity.

Also, the subpoena should have a list of documents that are being requested. Review that list carefully in case some items are personal and not relevant to your case.

Can I stop my ex from subpoenaing my bank accounts?

You probably are not going to be able to stop your ex from subpoenaing your bank account. You may, however, be able to ask to have specific information excluded. You may also be able to work with your bank to have some information redacted[9] from the statements. For instance, if your ex only asked for "deposits" in the request, then none of your withdrawals would be relevant or necessary to disclose.

How do I know who to serve the subpoena to at a bank or other business?

You can look up who to serve via the internet. Most businesses are required to list an agent who will accept service on behalf of the company.

Can I stop my ex from subpoenaing doctor's or counselor's records?

Again, it depends. Usually, a doctor or counselor will not release patient records without a HIPAA release signed by the patient for the records being requested. However, if you are having a custody battle and your physical or mental health is at issue, you may be required to sign a HIPAA release. If you are going to sign a HIPAA release, be sure to review what documents are being requested. Your ex should probably not have access to ALL your medical records since the time you were born. Documents should be provided for a specific span of time and maybe for only specific issues. For instance, gynecology records may not be relevant. Also, you may want to request that the doctor only release documents that are pertinent to your mental or physical health and ability to care for your child.

Am I required to provide my ex with copies of everything I receive from a subpoena?

Yes, not only are you required to provide them with a copy of the subpoena when you send it out, you are also required to provide them with a copy of the documents you receive. Your court may also have a time requirement for when you must provide your ex with a copy of the documents.

NOTE
Even if you think your ex already has the documents you received from the subpoena, you must still provide a complete copy of what you receive. If you would like to bates[10] stamp them before providing the documents to the opposing side, that would be helpful for everyone.

---

[9] Redacted means edited to limit what the receiver can actually see.
[10] Bates stamping is where you add an identifying mark to each page. For instance, if my client's name is John Smith, I might mark my documents with JSmith0001, JSmith0002. This can be done easily by using the Adobe program. However, you can also hand write

Interview

Interviewing witnesses is a really good way to make sure you know what they will testify to. An interview is much different than a deposition. The witness being interviewed will not be under oath when speaking with you and the witness is not required to speak to you.

Be careful when you attempt to interview a witness. You want to be sure not to harass the witness. If the witness refuses to take or return your calls, texts or emails just make a note of it and you can ask them about it in court. Since the witness is not required to speak to you, it is unlikely he will actually be willing to do so. In family law cases, it's pretty rare to have the opposing party's fact witness be willing to be informally interviewed.

If you are lucky enough to have someone willing to speak with you, the purpose is to find out what they are going to be speaking about. For instance, if your ex's sister is going to testify, you will want to ask her what your ex asked her sister to testify about. Don't try to argue your case. If she has some facts wrong you can ask her if she would like to know the truth. Be sure you do not harass her to try to get her to change her testimony. You do not want to be in trouble for interfering with or harassing a witness.

Request for Admissions

Some states allow a party to send a Request for Admissions to the opposing party, in order to gather specific information. A request for admissions is just like it sounds. You can write a question, such as: "Admit you were arrested for DUI in 2021" and sent it to the other party to answer. If the person admits it, you have saved yourself some time because you can have it admitted as an exhibit. You may be limited to the number of questions you can ask.

EXAMPLE
1. Admit you were arrested for DUI in 2021.
Admit_____Deny _____

---

the numbers on the bottom of the documents. This makes it easy for the court and witnesses to identify which document you are talking about.

> 2. Admit you plead guilty to Domestic Violence in 2020.
>
> Admit_____ Deny _____

The request for admissions should appear on a pleading with the questions listed and numbered. Under the questions you should leave space for your ex to write the answers.

What if my ex refuses to answer the questions in the Request for Admissions?

If your local rules permit the use of Request for Admissions, they will also likely have a deadline by which the response must be provided. In Arizona if the response is not timely provided, the questions are presumed to be admitted.

What if the answer is not yes or no or needs an explanation?

If you need to provide an explanation you can. For instance, if you were asked if you were arrested for DUI that does not mean you were convicted. So, you could say True with an explanation that the case was dropped because you were not intoxicated. But remember, the more words you write down, the more evidence that is available to be used against you.

Request for Production of Documents and Things

When you want to require the other party to produce documents or recordings or really anything to be used as evidence, you can send them a request. In Arizona that request is called "Request for Production of Documents and Things". Different jurisdictions have different names. California calls it a "Request for Production of Documents and/or Inspection of Places or Things". The name is not as important as what it allows you to gather. Follow the guidance of the rules in your jurisdiction.

If your ex has possession of all of the financial records, you may need to ask for production in order to know the total marital assets and debts. If your ex has told you that she recorded you screaming at the kids, you can ask for a copy of all recordings from a specific time period. If your ex kept a journal and has disclosed just one page, you can ask her to disclose the entire journal.

If your ex has a business, or you own a joint business, but are unable to obtain documents necessary to determine the value of the business, you may want to request the bank statements, profit loss statements, general ledger, K-1s or tax returns, outstanding receivables, invoices, purchase orders, inventory, client list, website analytics, and any other document you can think of.

Sometimes parties will exchange documents without the need for a formal "request". However, it is better to be safe than sorry, so prepare the formal request. Also, make sure you put the due date on the calendar. After you serve[11] a copy of the request for production, the opposing party will have a limited number of days by which to respond. Check your local rules to determine the amount of time. After the allotted time has passed, you should send a letter or email stating that the time has passed and ask to be provided by a specific deadline. If you ex does not provide the documents by the new "deadline", you may be required to request the court compel your ex to provide the requested documents. You can make the request by filing a motion. Some courts might want you to just reach out to the judge and see if she can intervene to get it done. Even within the same court system, judges may have their own preferences.

What happens if my ex refuses to provide the requested documents?

Each jurisdiction has its own rules for compelling a party to comply with discovery requests. Some jurisdictions will even sanction[12] the other party for not appropriately complying with the rules of the court and the discovery requests. The court can then order the other party to comply by a certain date. If that party still refuses to comply, the court may appoint a Special Master or other designated person to oversee the completion of discovery requests. Finally, if the person still fails to provide the requested discovery the court can either make a negative inference or you can ask the court to hold the other party in contempt. You can also ask the court to be sure to add in the decree that any other undisclosed or assets discovered after trial that were not divided by the court in the final order would be equally divided if uncovered. You could also ask the court to permit you to continue to do discovery even after the divorce is final, which would allow you to continue doing discovery.

How do I keep track of all the documents to make sure the other party provided everything I have asked for?

---

[11] You will need to make sure you serve the document in accordance to the rules. However, once litigation has started, many jurisdictions will permit you to serve discovery requests via mail, email, or hand delivery. But check your local rules to be sure.
[12] Sanction is a penalty the court may give to a party refusing to follow court rules or orders. Usually, sanctions consist of attorney fees and litigation costs.

I recommend you create a table of all the documents you requested, the date requested, anything provided and the date provided.

Request	Req Date	Provided	Date Rec'd	Notes
Bank Acct xxx – 2016 - 2021	3/5/21	All months	4/2/21	
Bank Acct xxx – 2017 - 2021	3/5/21	January 2017-July 2017 and Sept 2017– Nov 2017 All 2018 All 2019	4/7/21	NEED August and December 2017 All 2020 All 2021
ABC co 2017 - 2020 tax returns	3/5/21			Nothing provided
Recordings of DV 6/2/20	3/5/21			Not provided

Or you can simply prepare a really long list of what was requested. This will be a long list, but it will be on your computer and easy to update. It is important to keep track of what is outstanding.

EXAMPLE

March 5, 2021 Request

Bank request for XXX 2017
_____January
_____February
_____March
_____April
_____May
_____June
_____July

Tax returns and attachments
_____2020
_____2021

April 7, 2021 Request
_____Recording of DV

There is no hard and fast rule for keeping track of discovery, but it is important to be sure that you do keep track of it. When you have requested a lot of discovery, it is easy to miss something that has been provided. It is also easy to not notice what has not been provided. If you do not realize that documents were never provided until a week before trial, you may be out of luck.

> **NOTE**
>
> I have seen people purposefully omit one or two months out of a year's worth of bank statements because they had a big deposit or big withdraw or both. It is important to make sure that every single month of bank statements is accounted for if you believe there to be any hidden money.
>
> As soon as you receive the discovery, you should go through it to ensure everything has been provided.

As soon as you realize you have not received the requested discovery by the due date, you should reach out to the opposing party or opposing counsel and make them aware of the deficiency. It is important to follow-up and to make a good faith effort to obtain the discovery without court intervention. However, if you cannot resolve the issues, that is the time to seek court intervention.

Discovery requests served upon you.

If the other party serves you with discovery requests, you will likely be required to comply with their request. Check your rules for service requirements and exceptions. If you feel like you really don't want to give up some information and you do not believe you should be required to give up the information, you may want to consult an attorney in your area and ask for help objecting to the request and seeking a protective order or review the rules carefully if you want to object yourself. If your local rules permit you to file a motion for a protective order, you may want to do that. If granted, the protective order is an order that protects you from being required to provide at least some requested documentation. Be sure to follow the rules and be sure to let the court know exactly why you should not be required to provide the documents.

Is there any alternative to providing the documents to my ex? I'm afraid he will show other people the documents.

You may be able to request an in-camera review of your documents. That means only the judge would be permitted to see the documents. You can also request that only the lawyer be permitted to see the documents that were disclosed.

If legal decision-making and parenting time is at issue, then mental health records, arrest records, rehab records, etc. are fair game. However, if you believe your ex will share that information with others, and you have proof that your ex has done that before, you may want to request the judge block him from seeing the information. Furthermore, if the issue is only about child issues, your life insurance records, stock purchases and the like may not be fair game if it is a paternity or post decree issue.

If Spousal Maintenance/Child Support/Division of Property or Enforcement is at issue then your bank accounts are usually fair game. If this is post decree and modification of support is at issue, your bank statements and credit card statements are probably fair game; especially if you are self-employed or have failed to make payments previously ordered by the court. If there is a new spouse, their bank records and credit card statements may also be at issue. Talk to a lawyer if you want to protect your spouse's bank statements.

Interviews

If the opposing party lists witnesses, they should be providing their names and contact information and what that witness will testify about. Although you may call them or email them and ask to speak with them, unless there is an order prohibiting you from doing so, you do not have the right to harass them and they are not required to speak to you. If it is an important witness, you may wish to depose them. Not all courts will allow you to depose witnesses who are not parties to the case. However, if you can show good cause as to why you need to depose them, the court may allow it.

Furthermore, if you attempted to interview the witness but the witness refused, you may want to bring that up to the Judge.

Subpoenas

Subpoenas can be used to gather information. For instance, if you are trying to get your ex's credit card statements or bank statements, subpoenas are perfect for that. They are also helpful in obtaining counseling records or doctor's records. However, if you are trying to obtain you ex's records you will likely need to have your ex sign a HIPAA release. There may be a court fee associated with getting a subpoena and there may also be costs associated with getting copies of the requested documents.

- Who to Serve - You will either need to call the company you wish to subpoena and ask who you serve or look up the company name on the corporation commission or your state's Secretary of State and see who is listed as the person to serve.

- Out of Town Service - If you are trying to serve someone outside of your state, you may need someone in that state to help get you a subpoena domesticated and served in that state. However, many companies will comply without forcing you to jump through hoops. But some companies will not.

- Bank Records - If you are trying to obtain bank records, you may end up being required to provide the banks with more information, such as your ex's social security number, birth date and the like.
    - You will want to request any and all statements for any and all accounts for some period of time, such as from January 1, 2017 to December 31, 2019.
    - If you want signatures cards or information from when the accounts were opened, make sure to ask for those specific items.

Protective Order

Protective Orders are different from Orders of Protection. Protective Orders are used if you do not believe you should be required to provide certain documents or answer certain questions, and the other side is trying to force it; if that is the case, look up your local rules on protective orders. You may be able to obtain a protective order. A protective order is a tool used to protect privileged information or help a person who is being harassed by discovery requests.

Although there is a lot of leeway granted during discovery, you may still have the right to protect some information. For instance, if opposing counsel tries to get a copy of your hard drive from your computer, you may have the right to ask the court to protect it if it has attorney client privileged information on it. You may also have proprietary business information on the computer.

Opposing counsel will likely be able to get information on your income and, if you have children, your mental health. However, you might be able to get a protective order if they go after your gynecology records. You might also be able to protect trade secrets or other confidential documentation.

How to use your discovery.

You can use the information you received during discovery in a couple of different ways. For instance, you can use the interrogatory answers you received during a deposition. For example, if your ex lied on the interrogatories, you may want to bring that up in a deposition. However, if you do have good proof that he lied, you may want to wait until trial to use it.

You can also use your discovery to help you find other documents that might be helpful to your case. For example, if you see that money was transferred to a different bank, you may want to subpoena that bank to determine where the money went.

Disclosure

Disclosure is evidence that you intend to use in court. It can be pictures, recordings, and documents. You must timely provide the other side with any documents you want to use in court. As you can see, I stated the evidence must be "timely" disclosed. In some jurisdictions if you do not provide the other side with your disclosure by the dates and time mandated by the court, you may lose your right to use that evidence in court.

There may be some strategic reasons to hold off disclosing your documents until the due date, but those strategic reasons are few and far between. Get your evidence disclosed so you do not lose your right to use it.

Make sure you have a record of when each item was disclosed and how it was disclosed. I keep a running list of my disclosures. I have had attorneys state in court that they did not receive certain disclosure. I was able to prove them wrong. It not only made me look good, but also made the other attorney look unprepared.

You may disclose documents on several different dates. So, you will have something like Petitioners First Disclosure Statement, the Petitioner's Second Disclosure Statement, etc. When you prepare the statements, it is really helpful to keep everything from the previous disclosure statement on the next disclosure statement with a statement that all changes to your disclosure statement will be bolded. Then at the end of the disclosure statement, you can add a statement that says something like this:

It is assumed you have received all documents listed in this disclosure statement. If for any reason you believe you have not received all previous disclosure, please contact me as soon as possible so I can ensure you have all documentation.

Try to protect yourself along the way. It can really come in handy to be organized with your disclosures and may be helpful to arrange the disclosure in a table such as the one below.

Disc #	Bates #	Description of Disclosure	Date Disclosed
1	CR0001	Kelly Blue Book Value for Chevy	August 15, 2021
2	CR0002 – CR0018	Appraisal of Marital home 1111 N. 1st Street	August 15, 2021
3	CR0019 – CR0023	Appraisal of Artwork in house	September 8, 2021
4	CR0024 – CR0136	Bank Statements from January 2020 – December 2020	October 1, 2021

Also, when you update your list, do a "save as" and keep the previous disclosure statements as proof. It is also helpful to keep any emails in which you attached your disclosure statement.

Required Disclosure

Most, if not all courts have rules for required disclosure. You should be sure to check the rules to see what the required disclosure is. The court rules may require that you disclose some items even if you do not want to use them, such as tax returns, W2s, pay stubs, and the like.

You will also be required to disclose any documents you intend to use in court. Unlike television, you typically do not get to hide evidence and then spring it on the other party in court.

Disclosure Statement

Most, if not all, courts have rules for disclosure statements. They may just want a financial disclosure statement or they may want a disclosure statement that addresses everything from finances to custody. Be honest and be thorough. You don't want to lie on your disclosure statement only to have the court find out.

If the court finds out you lied about one thing, they may believe you lied about everything.

Judges have a lot of discretion when dividing assets/debts, awarding custody and parenting time and awarding attorney fees. If a judge simply does not like you, her discretion may lean favorably to your ex. It is important to always act respectful to the judge and her staff.

Extra Disclosure

This is all the evidence you will want to provide to the court to back up your story. If your ex is hiding money, you want documents to show that. If your ex has been abusive and you have photos and emails to prove it, you will want to disclose those. If your ex has a DUI or was in rehab, you will want to disclose that information as well.

IMPORTANT DISCLOSURE NOTE

If you disclose part of your journal or calendar, the entire journal or calendar could come into evidence. Keep that in mind. It is rare that you will want your entire journal disclosed unless you only journaled when your ex was being a jerk. But be very careful with your disclosures.

Fact Witnesses

If you want someone to come into court and testify on your behalf, they will need to be disclosed. They also may require you to subpoena them. Make sure your witnesses are either willing to come or that you subpoena them if they are not. For instance, teachers and counselors usually require subpoenas, so do police officers.

When you disclose your witnesses, you will need to disclose their names, addresses, and phone numbers. You will also need to disclose what that witness will testify to. For instance, if your ex assaulted you and you called the police, you might disclose that the police officer will testify as to what he saw when he arrived at your home and what his found during his investigation.

If you have family members that witnessed abuse or inappropriate behavior, make sure you state what inappropriate behavior was witnessed.

Expert Witnesses

An expert witness is a witness who is paid to come and testify as an expert about some portion of the case. For instance, a forensic accountant might testify about how your ex's tax returns are not accurate or that your ex is hiding money.

Expert witnesses may have to be disclosed sooner than other witnesses. It's good to disclose them as soon as possible to ensure the judge allows them to testify. You may also be required to disclose his curriculum vitae. Follow the disclosure rules in your area.

When disclosing this witness, be sure to provide her name, phone number, address and basic information about what she will testify about. If your expert provided a report, make sure you state that the expert will be discussing her report dated_____and disclosed_____.

Your court may have other rules regarding expert witnesses. For instance, you may not be permitted to reach out and talk to the other party's expert witness without permission or during a deposition.

Witness & Exhibit List

Some courts will require you to file a witness and exhibit list. Make sure you provide all the information as stated above. You may also be required to state what the witness or exhibit will be used for. You will need to file the list on pleading paper or at least on a document that has all the required information; such as case name, case number, title of document, name, address, and phone number of person filing the documents, a signature and the end and verification that the document has been provided to the other party and the means by which the document was provided.

List of Witnesses and Exhibits

FACT WITNESS

1. Cindy Walls (Petitioner)
   111 N. 5th Street
   San Fran, CA 91111
   202-202-2002
   Petitioner will testify to all issues before the court.

2. John Smith (Respondent)
   123 Main Street
   Oklahoma City, OK 12345
   101-101-1001
   Respondent will testify to all issues before the court.

3. Martha Fee
   9797 N 111 St
   Phx, AZ 85002
   606-606-6006
   Martha will testify that she saw Cindy Walls throw a brick and John Smith's car. She will also testify that she saw Cindy fall on the ground and at which time she hurt her right leg and her right upper arm.
   Witness was disclosed March 3, 2021.

EXPERT WITNESS

4. Dr. Johnson
   4549 W. Doctor Street
   Glendale, AZ 85011
   404-404-4004
   Dr. Johnson will testify regarding his opinion of Dr. Smith's custody evaluation report. Dr. Johnson will testify that Dr. Smith failed to meet the psychological standards by which custody evaluations should be conducted.
   Dr. Johnson will further opine as to what he believes Dr. Smith should have done and the probable outcome for recommendations had Dr. Smith followed the standards set by the APA and AFCC Guidelines.

Consulting Experts

If you hire an expert who simply helps you prepare for your case or cross examination of another expert, you may not be required to disclose him if he is not going to testify. Check the rules in for your court.

CHAPTER 11 – SETTLING OUTSIDE OF COURT

You should feel free to settle with your ex if you can. I like to discuss settlements with my clients before they enter them so I can inform them of the pros and cons, but it's your divorce, if you want to call up your ex and reach a settlement, that is great. If you do have an attorney, you should talk to him about the settlement, because there are definitely things to consider in your settlement.

- If you enter into an agreement, make sure it is in writing and signed by both parties.
- Make sure the agreement is fair and equitable or the court may not allow it.
- Make sure the agreement is in the best interest of the child or the court may not allow it.
- Make sure both parties were sober at the time of the agreement and able to enter into the agreement at the time.
- Do not blackmail or otherwise coerce your ex into entering into an agreement.
    o You are allowed to let them know what you will be seeking if you do not enter into an agreement. But you are not allowed to say that you will call the cops for the domestic violence if they don't enter the agreement. That doesn't mean you can't call the cops and make reports, you just can't threaten to if the other party refuses to agree.

Remember, you will be stuck with this agreement. If you are not happy with it, or at least ok with it, do not enter into it. It may be difficult to get out of a signed agreement. Check the rules in your jurisdiction to determine when it will be possible to seek modification.

Mediation

A mediation is an intervention between conflicting parties to promote settlement or compromise. A mediation may be free (through the court) or you may be required to pay for a private mediator. You can attend the mediation with or without an attorney. Some people have an attorney on call which can help save money.

Settling during a mediation may offer you things that a judge cannot or will not order. For instance, a court may not be willing or able to make any orders requiring a spouse leave the other spouse as the beneficiary for their life insurance policy, However, you can make those agreements in a mediation.

It's important to know what is most important to you. For instance, if having more parenting time is more important than spousal maintenance, you can bargain away your right to receive spousal maintenance. If you would be the payor of spousal maintenance and you are adamant about not paying your ex monthly payments, you can offer to give your ex a disproportionately larger share of cash, retirement funds, equitable offset of property or you can take more debt. When you settle your case in mediation you can be really creative. It is important that you have a mediator who is creative and has significant experience.

It is also important that both sides have completed discovery to ensure you can enter into a fair and equitable settlement. If you do not know values of businesses or homes or vehicles or retirement, how will you know how to divide the assets and debt?

One issue that regularly arises during a deposition is what will happen to the marital home. For instance, if both parties want to buy the house, how can that be resolved; or if one party wants to live in the house until the kids are 18, what does that look like. If the parties agree one person will have the house, they must also determine the value.

One thing to remember is to put deadlines for any agreement that requires an action. For instance, a deadline might be necessary for refinancing a house or paying a party an equitable offset. You may also want to be sure to make consequences if someone does not do what they are required to do by the deadline. For instance, if Party A was required to refinance the marital home by July 2021, but July 2021 has come and gone and the house has not been refinanced, what should happen? Maybe the house gets put up for sale. If that happens, who receives the equity? If someone does not pay an amount by the required time, does interest kick in; might they receive a judgment?

Mediation is the perfect time to be creative for every aspect of the divorce.

Mediators

Mediators are trained to help parties settle their cases in a fair and equitable manner. Mediators may conduct their mediations via Zoom, or in their office conference rooms, or at one of the attorney's offices. Zoom seems to be the most preferred method. However, if you prefer to meet in person, just ask your mediator. If you want to be sure you are not in the same room as your ex, for any reason, let your mediator know that.

If there has been significant domestic violence, mediation may be difficult. If the mediation is in person, the victim may want to ask what policies are in place to protect the victim. If the mediator does not have protective policies in place, a Zoom mediation might be a better idea.

Prior to attending a mediation, you should know what your bottom line is or what you are willing to settle for. You may want to meet with an attorney to help you understand the laws and possible or even probable outcomes if the case goes to trial. For instance, if you want to have sole legal decision-making and you want your ex to have minimal parenting time, you may be willing to settle for sole legal decision-making but 50/50 parenting time.

Who May Attend the Mediation?

The mediator will typically determine who is permitted to attend the mediation. Most mediators do not permit new significant others to attend mediations. Sometimes the parties wish to have their parents attend or a good friend. You should ask the mediator prior to bringing someone into the mediation. Sometimes friends and family do more harm than good when they attend the mediation. It might be better just to have them available on the phone or to text.

Sometimes it is helpful to have experts attend the mediation. The experts can help the mediator understand what they will testify to, which can help the parties settle. Forensic accountants are often brought to mediations to help the mediator understand how the value of a business was determined or how hidden money was found.

Interpreter

If English is your second language, you may want to ask the mediator to have an interpreter available for the mediation. It is important for both parties to completely understand the agreement for it to be enforceable.

Choosing a Mediator

You may want to choose a mediator based on cost, experience, personality, services provided, recommendations or all of the above. Mediators are not required to be attorneys. Most states just require mediators to take a 30–40-hour course and spend some amount of time as an apprentice.

Costs

Mediators can be retired judges, attorneys or non-lawyers who took a course to become a mediator. Because the types and experience of mediators can vary so much, the cost of mediators also varies dramatically. An attorney who is a family law specialist, may charge up to $1,000 per hour (depending on where you live), whereas someone who simply took the mediation course may charge $50 or less. Typically, the cost of mediation is split between the parties. If both parties pay, they both seem to take it more seriously. When only one party pays the other party often has little desire to settle and might rather run up the bill.

If you to want the best chance of your mediation being successful, you should choose a mediator who has significant experience with family law cases in your area.

Experience

Experience is important if you want your mediation to be successful. When you have an experienced mediator helping you settle, you are much more likely to reach a complete agreement. That is because an experienced mediator understands what the court is most likely to do in certain situations. Furthermore, an experienced mediator can be very creative when making suggestions that can help the parties settle. Finally, you will want a mediator who is familiar with the statutory laws and the case laws. A mediator with that type of experience can be very persuasive when helping to create settlements which the parties are likely to adopt.

Personality

It is important to have a mediator with a personality that will work with both of the parties. For instance, if one party does not respect women, it might not be helpful to have a woman mediator. That doesn't mean it's right and that doesn't mean it is ok to disrespect women, it simply means if the parties want to settle, finding someone with a personality that is a good fit for both parties works best.

Services Provided

Some mediators are willing to provide not only mediation services, some are also willing to file all necessary documents if the parties agree[13].

Not all mediators are willing to file papers. If you want a mediator to also file papers, be sure to ask prior to hiring a mediator. When choosing a mediator, be sure to do your homework to ensure you end up with a skilled mediator. The mediator can make or break your mediation.

Confidential Mediation Memorandum

A Confidential Mediation Memorandum is a document created by each party that provides settlement information to your mediator. The Memorandum should contain information on all issues that are before the court along with your position on all issues.

You should prepare a Memorandum and provide it to the mediator prior to the mediation. The mediator will typically send an engagement letter that will provide the details of the mediation, give a deadline for the Memorandum and tell you whether it is "confidential". If the mediator does not indicate whether it is confidential, you should probably ask to be sure.

Having a thorough Memorandum can help the mediator settle your case. Memorandums should contain exactly what you want to get out of the mediation. For instance, you should be specific about what you want in your parenting plan. If you have special holiday requests or drop of and pick up requests, make sure the requests are in the memorandum.

What should I bring to the mediation?

Mediations can be long and exhausting. I always recommend clients bring water, a snack, paper to take notes, their file (preferably via computer), and exhibits that can help a mediator understand certain issues. For instance, if you are trying to prove a waste claim, you should bring the documents that show marital waste. Those may be bank statements that show large transfers or

---

[13] Some mediators will file the Petition and Response, some will file the settlement agreement

charges for trips where your ex took his girlfriend. When you provide solid proof to support your allegations, your mediator can take those exhibits to the other side and explain what he thinks will happen in regard to that issue. The more ammunition you bring to the mediation, the easier it will be for the mediator to convince your ex that you have a great case.

Settlement Conference

A settlement conference may be the same as a mediation in some states or it may be a little different. Either way, it is a means by which to reach an agreement. Sometimes the court will order a Settlement Conference with a judge actually acting as the Settlement Conference Officer. If that is the case, you will still want to follow most of the rules for mediation.

If your judge is the person conducting the mediation, be careful. You will really need to be on your best behavior. You may also be asked to waive any conflict that may occur if the judge doing the mediation is going to be your judge at trial. That is because the judge will be hearing evidence that may not be admissible in court and which could affect his ruling if you don't settle all the issues. For instance, if you tell the judge you are unwilling to waive a civil suit because your ex gave you herpes, that may make the judge not like the opposing party. In court that may not have been admissible. Furthermore, if you are acting unreasonable and not following the law, the judge may not like you. Judges have so much discretion with their orders that you really do want the judge to like you. If you can respectfully express your reservations about having the same judge doing your trial that is doing the mediation, you may wish to strongly consider making such a request.

Alternative Dispute Resolution (ADR)

ADR is any means to reach resolution without having to attend litigation. Therefore, ADR can be a mediation, a settlement conference, a meeting between the parties with or without attorneys, or arbitration. Though arbitration is a form of litigation. Which form of ADR that is ordered will depend on your jurisdiction and your court requirements.

Arbitration

Arbitration is much like a private judge; however, they have specific and different rules which they must follow. Each state has their own arbitration rules. However, you will likely be required to provide evidence, just as you would for trial. However, you will need to be careful when deciding if you will waive certain rights by arbitrating as opposed to going to trial.

Private Judge

A private judge is a judge who the parties agree to hire to hear their case and make rulings. Each state has its own rules for whether or not parties can hire a private judge; if their use is permitted, those states also have rules for what that will look like.

Why do people want to spend money to hire a private judge when court will provide one for free?

There are several reasons parties might want to hire a private judge:

- Parties do not want to wait. Sometimes judges set hearing out for several months after the parties are ready to proceed. If the parties want the process to move more quickly, a private judge might be the way to go.

- Trial Time Constraints. Some courts only provide a small amount of time for each trial to take place and some people believe they need more time. If the state or county court will only provide three hours for a trial and you think you need two days, you might want to look into hiring a private judge.

- Privacy. Some people who divorce want to ensure their privacy. Divorce courts, unless otherwise ordered, are usually open to the public. Celebrities are often willing to pay for a private judge to keep their case out of the public's eye.

- Complicated case. Many jurisdictions have judges that rotate to different areas of court. For instance, a judge may be on the criminal court bench for three years, then get transferred to family court. That judge may have only minimal experience handling family law cases. Furthermore, the judge may not know the rules or how to control his court. If you have a very complicated case, hiring a judge may be a really good idea.

- Terrible Judge. Some judges are not great at their jobs. If a jurisdiction does not permit you to get rid of a judge, you may be stuck with a problem judge. In some jurisdictions judges are appointed and other jurisdictions they are voted in. When a judge is appointed by the governor it is really difficult to get them off the bench.

Cost will vary between locations and experience. There are many very skilled private judges across the country. If you decide to look for a private judge, see if you can find some recommendation.

Meet and Confer

Most courts want you to have some sort of conference with the opposing side. The court wants to see if there is anything you can agree to. However, the courts may not require you to attend such a conference if neither of you are represented.

If you do meet with the other party to try to settle some issues, it would be good for you to reach at least some small agreements if at all possible. When you go to court and let the court know that you did reach a couple agreements, the court will feel like you tried and that you may be reasonable.

Settlement Offers Between Parties

I wholeheartedly believe parties should try to settle between themselves. I believe this for several reasons. First, it will save time and money if you reach a settlement prior to preparing for and going to court and or prior to having to pay a mediator. It will also help foster a better co-parent relationship. Settling without court intervention also allows you more flexibility in all areas. For instance, some courts may just divide everything in half or force you to sell property. When you work with each other, you can give and take and trade one asset for another and you can offset debts with assets. But it is also important to not let yourself be bullied into an agreement.

You will definitely want know what assets and debts exist that are subject to division; therefore, you should complete discovery prior to entering into agreements. I rarely recommend settling before all discovery is completed. If you do settle, you may find out that you got the raw end of the deal. If your ex is telling you that you do not have rights to something, you should speak with an attorney. You may have an equitable interest in your ex's separate property. You may also have an interest in your ex's retirement. You should also remember that your ex is likely not trying to help you even though she may be acting like she is.

CHAPTER 12 – PREPARING FOR COURT

Trial Preparation

It is important to prepare for your trial on many different levels. You need to prepare yourself for trial, you need to prepare your testimony for trial, you need to prepare your witnesses for trial, and you need to prepare your exhibits for trial and you need to know when your local rules or the court require you to file your trial exhibits with the court prior to trial.

Presenting Your Best Self for Trial

What does presenting your best self really mean? It means you should look the part and act the part of the person you want to project. Projecting a specific image will require insight and willingness to really dig deep. Projecting that image may actually require you to *fake-it-'til-you-make-it*. You may be afraid but you will have to act strong. You may be anxious but you will have to be brave and appear calm.

No matter how prepared you think your case is, unless you have been in court countless numbers of times, you need to spend time prepping yourself and possibly your witnesses.

Know Your Goal

I assume the purpose or your goal for going to trial is to have the judge make the orders that you want. Keep that in mind during the entire trial prep and even throughout the trial. The judges have a lot of discretion and given the same evidence two different judges could make two different findings and two different orders. With that much discretion, you really want the judge to like you more than he likes the opposing party. You want to make it easy for the judge to rule in your favor. Hand him the case on a silver platter if you can.

One to two weeks before trial

I like to have clients start preparing themselves for their appearance in court at least two weeks ahead of time. Since you may also be preparing your case, you will need to be preparing that much sooner than two weeks.

If you are going to get a haircut before trial, this is the time to do it. Let's face it, if you don't feel like you look your best, you may not actually do your best.

Having your hair done one to two weeks before trial will allow you to determine how best to wear your new haircut in a way that will make you feel confident.

If you are going to wear clothes that you already have, either take them to the cleaners or make sure they are clean and ready to go. If you are going to purchase a new outfit, now is the time to do that. Make sure the outfit you purchase follows the guidelines below.

- Clothing should cover tattoos. I understand that many many people have tattoos. Even your judge may have a tattoo. However, you want to be sure to appeal to the largest audience. Therefore, I recommend covering tattoos if possible.

- When choosing the colors for your outfit, you need to decide what attitude and personality you are trying to present to the court. If you want the court to think you are kind and gentle and not a bully or harsh, you should consider wearing soft colors, pastels, or cream, or white.
    - When you are choosing an outfit, be sure you have shoes to go with your outfit/suit. If you never wear heals, this is not the time to try. But you should have clean shoes.

- If you need childcare for when you are at your hearing, find someone now so you are not stressed about it later. It is important to plan what you can ahead of time to ease anxiety and nerves.

- If you are extremely nervous about the hearing, think about observing a hearing. You can either observe a hearing in the same court with the same judge, or you can observe a hearing in a different court by a different judge. You may want to even attend a few hearings so you can see how different people present their cases. This might give you an opportunity to see how lawyers present their cases. Trials and hearings are not really like what you see on television.

One week before trial

If you are representing yourself, you have probably been reviewing the exhibits throughout the case. However, if you are represented by counsel and/or if you have not recently reviewed the exhibits, do so now.

If you have prepared a *prehearing statement, affidavit or declaration* you should review it at this time. If you haven't prepared one, check the rules to see if they are permitted and/or if you still have time to submit one. If you have one prepared, be sure to review it and even make notes.

If your ex prepared a statement for the court, it might be really helpful for you to review it and makes notes about any statements that are untrue. If you have proof that the statements are untrue, try to get that proof before the court, especially if you have documents or recordings that show dishonesty.

If you do have an attorney, you should email any questions you may have to your attorney at this time.

You should review the order setting the trial to confirm the date, time and location of hearing. If you do have an attorney, you will want to confirm where you will meet your attorney and how early your attorney wants you there. You should also Google Maps the drive to the court at for the same day and time as the hearing to determine the drive time.

Three days before trial

It's getting close to trial; you want to make sure everything is ready.

- Confirm childcare if necessary.
- Pick up clothes from dry cleaners.
- Make sure you have the directions to the court.
- Make sure you have all your necessary documents
- Make sure you have your ex's exhibits to review.

Day before trial

You may be getting anxious and worried. I suggest you use lavender and do whatever you can to relax. Being over-prepared (if there even is such a thing) is the best way to help calm your nerves. Below are more suggestions to help you prepare and be calm.

- Lay out clothes for trial
- Eat nutritious food the day before, you may not feel like eating tomorrow.
- Exercise if possible. Exercise is the best way to help you relax and to stop anxiety.
- Confirm childcare. I cannot emphasize this enough. You don't want to be thinking about how to care for your kids the morning of trial.

- Review exhibits one more time. If you feel up to it, just flip through the exhibits one more time. If not, then be done.
- Review Prehearing Statement. Just a quick look might help.
- Try to get 8 hours of sleep.

Day of hearing

On the day of the hearing, do whatever you can to calm your nerves. If you do yoga or run or regularly exercise, try to wake up early enough to do that.

- Eat a healthy meal before your hearing. You may not feel up to it, but at least try to take a bite.
- Be early to court. You don't want to have the extra stress of being late.
- Coffee…. I usually recommend that my clients not use coffee. However, if you are presenting the case by yourself, you may need it. I'd limit the caffeine if you can.

Appearance

Appearance matters. We don't always want to think that anyone is judging us on how we look, but they absolutely do. If you look unkept, the court might think you take care of your children the same way. I am not saying that any one person is better than someone else because of the he or she looks. However, I am saying that all people have biases, even judges. My recommendations regarding your appearance are to help you appeal to the largest audience. For instance, some people might say that a person with tattoos all over looks like a biker or a gang banger, and that presumption may be used against them. However, it is rare, in my opinion, that a person with tattoos would think less of someone without them.

- Hair should be neatly brushed/combed. If you tend to fiddle with your hair, pull it back.
- Make-up should be light. No dark red lips or smoky eyes.
    - Men should not wear make-up. I do not want to get into whether or not a man has the right to wear make-up. Of course, a man has a right to wear make-up. However, you have one shot at impressing the judge. If the judge has a prejudice against men wearing make-up, you may ruin your case. Again, I understand you have the

right to do what you want to do. However, it could come back to bite you. Just keep that in mind when making decisions about your appearance.
- Minimal perfume. Err on the side of less.
    - You do not want to make people in the courtroom sick. Take a shower that morning or the night before and use deodorant so you don't smell.
- Cover up tattoos and remove all piercings except one set of earrings for women.
    - Again, there is no reason to rehash your rights to have tattoos or multiple piercings. You want to appeal to the largest audience. You do that by conforming to societal norms. Even if you believe tattoos and piercings are societal norms, they may not be for the judges in the court. Some judges are ultra conservative. That is who you want to appeal to, because a judge who is not conservative may not care either way.

Be on time

This is so important it deserves a section all to itself. What happens if you are late to court? There are several possibilities. The judge may wait for 15 minutes or so, then permit the opposing party to testify and present evidence. The judge may just cancel the hearing. However, you likely won't know which one will happen until it happens.

If for any reason you cannot be on time, make sure you call the court as soon as you know you won't be on the time and provide them with a reason. Some judges are real sticklers and will proceed without you. However, some judges may just reschedule. If you have asked for a continuance before and it was denied, the court really might only continue the hearing if you are in the hospital or an accident. You may be required to provide proof of the problem. If you believe you have COVID symptoms, call your doctor. You want to have some evidence of your illness.

Attitude

When judges decide cases, they not only consider documents and other evidence that is admitted, but they also consider your demeanor and your credibility. The judge and her staff will usually watch you pretty closely.

Make sure you are professional and courteous to all people in the courtroom. Many courtrooms have cameras and microphones set up that may monitor the court, even when you aren't on the record. Do not get into a pissing match with the opposing party or opposing counsel. You need to keep your cool from before you even step into the courthouse until you are long gone from the parking lot. If you are a jerk to the security, the judge or their assistant, one of them may be nearby and witness your poor behavior. The courthouse staff all talk to each other. If you act like a jerk and someone sees your inappropriate behavior, the judge will likely find out. This is the time to fake it 'til you make it. Be kind and courteous to everyone when you are in court.

- Do not raise your voice
- Do not show any anger
- Be kind to every person you see that day.
- Do not give your ex the evil eye.
- Do not be condescending or snotty
- Do not be disrespectful to the judge.
- Do not cry hysterically

When it seems as if you are letting your emotions get the best of you, the judge may believe you will make decisions based on emotions rather than facts and/or the best interest of your child.

Evidence

Evidence is information you provide to the court to help prove what you want the court to know. Evidence can come in the form of testimony from you or another witness, documents or audio/video recordings. It is important that you only give the judge evidence that helps you in your case. Family law cases are often emotional and sometimes the parties want to tell the judge what a complete jerk the other party is. However, that may not be relevant to the issues. There may be time constraints so be sure to only use the evidence necessary to prove your case.

Disclosure

As stated above, it is important to provide the opposing party with any and all evidence you want to present at trial. Each jurisdiction has their own disclosure requirements. The deadline for disclosing an expert witness is likely going to be different than the deadline for disclosing a fact witness. If you do not disclose your evidence prior to the deadline, the court may not permit you to use the evidence. It is important to calendar deadlines.

When you receive an order or minute entry, be sure to review it carefully and calendar any deadlines. I used to put the deadlines a couple days before the real deadlines so I would never be late. When you calendar your deadlines[14], you should calendar reminders too. Otherwise, it is very easy to miss your deadlines.

Witness Testimony

There are different types of witnesses. There are expert witnesses, fact witnesses and character witnesses. An expert witness is someone hired by one of the parties or appointed by the court. A fact witness is a person who saw or heard something and is relaying what they saw or heard. A character witness is someone who is willing to testify about the character of one of the parties.

Make sure you choose witnesses that will best help your case. Make sure you speak with them and discuss their testimony. You need to know that they are going to say. However, if the court appoints an expert, be sure to review the order and/or rules to determine if there is a "no ex-parte" order. If there is, that means you are not permitted to speak to the expert witness without the other attorney or opposing side listening and/or participating in the interview.

Witnesses can be wishy washy. I have had witnesses tell me one thing, which I fully believed to be the truth; but when she was on the witness stand, she completely threw my client under the bus. She completely lied. If you think there is any chance of your witness doing that, you may want to record the interview.

Exhibits

There are different types of exhibits permitted in family court. You may use one type or you may use them all. You are not limited to just one type of exhibit. However, you may be responsible for appropriately presenting them to the court. This will be particularly important for video and audio recordings, demonstrative exhibits, and depositions. Do not expect the judge or the court to play your audio or video recordings unless you have confirmed with them that they are willing to do so.

Recordings

---

[14] The court may provide specific dates for deadlines or the court may say something like 2 weeks before court or 10 days before court. It is important to be accurate with your accounting.

Recordings can be a really great exhibit if done correctly. Check your court rules to see what, if any, specific requirements are in place regarding presenting a recording during the hearing.

If you have a recording that is 20 minutes long and you only want the court to hear 30 seconds of it. You will want to state specifically where in recording you want the court to listen. For instance, you might state in your prehearing statement:

The court should begin listening to the recording at the 10 minute 27 second mark and listen until the 10 minute 57 second mark.

You will also want to specify the section of time on the recording you are going to present on your exhibit list. That way the judge will not be required to listen to the entire recording. However, it is really important to know that the judge may listen to the entire recording. So, if that recording would do more harm than good if the judge listens to it in its entirety, you may want to rethink playing it. Also, if you submit the entire recording, the opposing party might decide to play the portions that are less favorable to you.

You will also be required to provide a means by which to play the audio or video recording. Check with the court to see what is available. Some courts have audio video connections available at the tables. However, some courts do not. You should plan ahead in case you need to bring a projector and screen or a tape player. Plan this out at least a couple weeks prior to trial. You do not want to get to trial and be totally unprepared. You also do not want to waste your trial time trying to get it to work.

If your court has audio video available for hook-up, you should ask the court or the clerk or the judicial assistant if you can come into the court when no one is there to practice setting it up.

NOTE
Be sure to read the rules of your court before trying to edit out any negative parts of the recordings. You may get in trouble for spoilation of evidence. The court may want to review the context in which the recording occurred.

Demonstrative Exhibits

A demonstrative exhibit is an exhibit that you create that sums up testimony or other exhibits.

Throughout this book I have provided examples of lists and tables that you should create to organize the division of property and the value of property. Those would be great documents to have to show the court the list of assets and debts and the division of them you would like to see the court order. You may also be able to add those tables and lists into your pretrial statement/declaration/affidavit[15].

If you are trying to show that your ex wasted money or spent joint money on a new girlfriend or boyfriend, it is also sometimes helpful to provide a document to the court showing withdrawals or transfers from a bank account. You will also want to have the bank statements available for the court and admitted into evidence so the judge can verify your entries.

You should disclose all demonstrative exhibits as soon as possible after you create them and your court rules may also have deadlines when they must be given to the court and/or the other side.

Depositions as Evidence

As stated above, when using depositions as evidence, the court may want to ensure they have a reliable and accurate document. Therefore, they may require you to provide a copy that is sealed and provided by the court reporter. You may also be required to disclose which parts of the deposition you want the judge to read. You can do that by "designating" the important portions. Even if this is not required, you may want to add the designations in a prehearing statement if permitted.

Pre-Trial

Pretrial Motions

Pretrial Motions are motions filed prior to the hearing. These motions may be heard before court starts or may be heard along with all the trial evidence. It is nice to get issues out of the way if possible.

Motions In Limine

A motion *in limine* is a request, outside the presence of the jury (if there is one), in which the parties will request testimony or evidence either be permitted

---

[15] A pretrial statement/affidavit is a document that you can provide the court that lays out all the issues before the court and your position on the issues.

or excluded prior to starting the trial. At this time, only one state, Texas, permits juries for the full divorce trial. Other states permit juries for some aspects of the divorce, but not for the entire process.

However, you can still file a motion in limine even if there is no jury. That motion will allow you to resolve the issue of whether evidence is coming in during the trial. By having a ruling on the motion prior to trial, that ensures valuable trial time will not be wasted arguing that about whether evidence can come in when you are in trial.

> ### EXAMPLE
>
> You want your ex's ex-girlfriends to testify about his angry, violent outbursts. Your ex of course wants that testimony excluded. Either one of you could file a motion in limine and request the judge rule on that issue prior to court.
>
> If you do not file that motion or if the judge does not rule before trial, that issue might not be resolved until the witness is sitting on the witness stand. It would be much more efficient if the judge were simply to rule on that prior to the start of the trial.

Motion for a witness to appear telephonically or by video

Witnesses are usually required to appear in person. If you have a witness who is unable or unwilling to attend court in person, you need to get permission from the court for that witness to appear telephonically or by video. To get permission, you usually need to file a motion allow the witness to appear telephonically. You will need to explain to the judge that your witness is unable or unwilling to appear in person, and the reasons. If it would be a financial hardship, or your client can't get child-care, state that in the motion. It might be helpful to attach a sworn, notarized affidavit from the witness to your motion.

It is really important to get permission for the telephonic appearance before the hearing. I have seen judges refuse to grant permission for a witness to appear by telephone or video made on the day of trial because the judge never received a written motion. Some judges may permit it, some judges may not.

If the judge does not permit your witness to appear telephonically, you will need to subpoena your witness to make her appear. Since COVID-19 all but shut down the courts, it has been much easier to get the judges to permit telephonic or video appearances. It appears that COVID is an excuse for so many things these days.

In the end, however, if you do not receive permission from the court for your witness to appear telephonically, that witness may very likely be excluded.

If you do *not* want a witness to appear telephonically, be sure to object. During your objection, you will need to provide the court with valid reasons for your objections. For instance, research shows that about 70 percent of communication is non-verbal. You and the court both should have the right to observe the witness's facial expressions and body language. Also, requiring the witness to appear in person would help to ensure that the witness is not being coached. Having the witness appear in person would help to ensure that the witness is in fact who she says she is.

Motion to close the courtroom

Many courtrooms are open to the public. If your jurisdiction permits the public to attend your divorce proceedings and if someone will be testifying to sensitive information, you may want to request the court close the courtroom and seal your records. "Sensitive information" might include someone's mental health issues, issues involving your child, proprietary business dealings and the like. The court may also consider closing the courtroom if you are prominent in the community.

If the court is normally open to the public, you will really need a good reason to cause the court to close the courtroom.

Motion to Seal

Most courts allow public access to court documents. They aren't always easy to get, but if someone knows how, they can legally obtain all the records in your case. Like closing the courtroom, the court will want you to have a good and valid reason to seal your case records. A reason to seal court records might be if you are famous and you fear the media or even the public will find and release personally sensitive information.

You can also request the court seal just individual documents. For instance, if mental health records are going to be part of the record, you may want to ask if the court will seal that specific document. You may need to actually file the document under seal at the same time you make the request. Otherwise, the request itself along with the arguments for sealing the record may end up as public records.

Motion for Summary Judgment

A Motion for Summary Judgment in family court, is a motion that is filed with the court to put one or two issues to rest[16]. This motion is used when the facts are not in dispute, but the laws, rules or probable outcome are in dispute. They are often used to get rid of a major issue in the case so the parties can either settle, or focus on other issues that will be going to trial.

For instance, if the law is clear that a second job "may" be counted as income for child support purposes, and one party has a second job and the other party wants that income included as income for child support purposes, one party may file a Motion for Summary Judgment to resolve that one issue.

Judges may just wait until trial to hear the issue. However, some judges may hear the issue if they believe it would be important to help you resolve the issue outside of court.

Statements/Affidavits/Memorandum/Declarations

Most courts will want you to prepare some document prior to your trial date that specifically lays out your case, facts, witnesses, and exhibits. If you are permitted to do this, do not take it lightly. This statement is extremely important. Check your rules and make sure you follow them. There may be page limits, you may be required to work with the opposing party to complete it, you may only be permitted to provide certain information. It is important to read the rules.

This document is important for a couple of reasons. First, it will help you prepare your case. You will be forced to organize your thoughts and your case and put them down on paper. Second, you can use it as an outline of your case to ensure you touch on every issue. And finally, after the judge hears all the evidence, she will likely take the matter under advisement. That means she will not give you a ruling from the bench and you will be required to wait for her to prepare an order. The judge may wait weeks or even months to prepare your order. Therefore, when the judge prepares the order, she will need to review all the exhibits that were admitted, she will review her notes, and she will review the statement you provided. If your statement is thorough and accurate, it will help refresh the judge's memory about your positions.

---

[16] Your motion can include a number of issues, however, if the judge is going to have a hearing on multiple issues, the judge may just wait for trial. That doesn't mean don't file for summary judgment on all issues, it just means don't add frivolous

Witnesses

Each side is permitted to call witnesses to help present their case. Once both sides disclose their witnesses, the other side is put on notice and should prepare questions to ask those witnesses at trial (cross examination).

However, it is important to understand that just because the opposing side has a witness listed, that does not mean they will be attending. Furthermore, even if that witness was subpoenaed by the other side does not mean that witness will attend the hearing. I have seen many attorneys subpoena a witness, then release them before they are required to testify. If you also wanted that witness to testify, you may be out of luck if he was released by the opposing party. The only way to ensure attendance of a witness at a hearing (even one listed by the other side) is to issue the subpoena to that witness yourself[17].

Witnesses appearing telephonically

As stated above, you are usually required to have the court's permission for a witness to appear telephonically. If the court has permitted you to have your witness appear telephonically, be sure to have that witnesses phone number available for the court. If you do not want the other party to have that number, be sure to write the number down on a piece of paper and provide it directly to the court. You also do not want to state the witnesses phone number on the record.

You should let your witness know approximately when to expect the court to call. You can usually guess if you know how many witnesses will be before her. If your witness only has a small window of time available, you may need to ask the court to take your witness out of order. (See more under Trial Procedures).

Subpoenas

In order to force a witness to testify, you will need to serve that witness with a subpoena to appear at a specific location at a specific time. Subpoenas were discussed more thoroughly above.

---

[17] If the witness does not appear after you have legally and appropriately subpoenaed him, you may need to seek court intervention to force his attendance.

CHAPTER 13 – TRIAL

Trial Procedure

Time Limits

It is important for you to know and understand what the time limits are for your case. If you are in a court with strict time limits you will need to use your time very wisely. I've seen attorneys and pro-se litigants ruin their chances of having a successful outcome because they wasted time on irrelevant issues.

You want to be sure to focus your testimony and the questions for your witnesses on relevant issues. If you waste time trying to make your ex look bad, you may not be able to get important information to the court. For instance, if it takes you 5 minutes to get your ex to admit he had an affair in a no-fault state, you just wasted 5 minutes, which could have been used to show he earned more than he is claiming or you could have saved it for a closing statement. Each minute you spend doing one thing is a minute less you have for something else.

Time Savers

- You can save time by being really familiar with your exhibits.
- You can save time by laying foundation for your exhibits to ensure fewer objections.
    - Foundation is formed by showing relevance, reliability and authenticity. An email from 30 years ago may not be relevant today, so you would want to provide the date as foundation. If you found a hand-written piece of paper that said something incriminating about your ex, you would want to state where you found it and if the you recognize the handwriting. Finally, the court will want the evidence to be reliable. Therefore, when you are seeking to have evidence admitted in trial, you want to state facts that show its reliability.
- You can save time by sticking to the relevant information.
- You can save time by having your questions or your testimony written out.

As I stated earlier, your jurisdiction has statutes which the court will follow to ensure consistency in the courts. I'm not saying judges are perfect at applying the rules and statutes, but it will help your case tremendously if you follow the guidance of the rules and statutes. You may however, need to at least have a consultation with a lawyer to be pointed in the right direction to find all the relevant statutes.

Order of Presentation of Case[18]
Each issue will be discussed in depth below the outline.

1. Housekeeping
2. Petitioner's Opening Statement[19]
3. Respondent's Opening Statement
4. Petitioner's Witnesses
    A. Direct Examination by Petitioner or Petitioner's counsel
    B. Cross Examination by Respondent or Respondent's counsel
    C. Redirect Examination by Petitioner or Petitioner's counsel
    D. The court may ask some questions then permit each side to ask questions based on the questions the court just asked.
5. Respondent's Witnesses
    A. Direct Examination by Respondent or Respondent's Counsel
    B. Cross Examination by Petitioner or Petitioner's counsel
    C. Redirect Examination by Respondent or Respondent's counsel
    D. The court may ask some questions then permit each side to ask questions based on the questions the court just asked.
6. Petitioner's Closing Argument
7. Respondent's Closing Argument
8. Petitioner may be permitted to have the last word.
9. Post-trial motions

You may need to have witnesses out of the order in which you planned to present them if they are not available or to save costs. If that is the case, you would want to ask the opposing party and or the court for permission.

Housekeeping

Housekeeping is what we call it when we (attorneys or litigants) need to take care of outstanding issues before we start the trial. So, if the judge enters the courtroom and wants to get started, you may need to say something like: Your Honor, just for housekeeping purposes, we still have two motions

---

[18] This order for case presentation is for your divorce trial. If the Respondent in a case filed a motion or requests some type of hearing, the Respondent should present her case first.
[19] Opening statements may not be permitted by the court and or you may not desire to do an opening statement.

outstanding that have not been ruled on. Or perhaps you might say, for housekeeping purposes, we would like to discuss the order of the witnesses.

In many cases there are pending motions which must be addressed prior to moving on to trail. The court may also set time limits. In Maricopa County, Arizona the judge place very strict limits on trial time. In fact, I have seen judges allow only 3 total hours (1.25 hours per side plus .5 for the court) for a full divorce trial with an expert witness. You need to plan accordingly and use your time wisely.

Other housekeeping matters might include, excluding witnesses from the courtroom or setting up the phone calls for witnesses who will appear telephonically, you will need to let the court know what number to call.

Opening Statements

Not all judges or courts allow opening statements. Furthermore, some jurisdictions only permit you to have a specified amount of time to put on your whole case. Any time you use for the opening statement is time you are unable to use somewhere else in your case. However, it is often worth it because it allows you to tell a story.

However, if your judge does allow an opening statement and that is how you want to spend your allotted time, be sure to follow these guidelines:

- Prepare it ahead of time. Don't "wing it". If you choose to "wing it" you are likely going to ramble.

- Keep it short and to the point.

- Be specific about what you want. If you want spousal maintenance, state exactly how much you want.

- State only facts that you will be able to prove.

- Mention specific exhibits and what the court will get out of it.

- Try to touch on each issue before the court.

- This Is not a time to be emotional. However, if you are a bit emotional (welled up eyes) that is okay.

> **EXAMPLE**
>
> *Your honor, today I am asking you to grant me Joint Legal Decision-Making with 50/50 parenting time. The evidence will show that I have been a very involved father and despite what respondent says, I have an appropriate place for the children to stay with me which is a 3-bedroom apartment in the kids' school district. Your honor I am also asking that you order the marital home sold and the proceeds equally divided. I am asking that I be reimbursed for expenses I paid for respondent after she was served with the divorce papers. I have an exhibit with the breakdown of all the expenses and how much was paid. I know respondent it looking for spousal maintenance, and I am asking the judge to deny spousal maintenance. This divorce has been ongoing for 2 years and she has refused to even look for a job. The evidence will show that she has her Ph.D in psychology and is capable of earning a very good income. Furthermore, we have only been married 8 years and it appears she is now looking for a free ride for another 8 years. Thank you. [then sit down]*

Petitioner's case

Typically, the person who filed for the divorce (Petitioner/Plaintiff) will put on his or her case first. In this case, I will assume you are the Petitioner.

Petitioner's direct examinations

A direct examination is when the litigant or his attorney questions his own witness to obtain testimony to support her case. The witness can be a fact witness or an expert witness.

The Petitioner will want to choose the order of the witnesses that will help her best present her case. For instance, you may want to have an expert witness testify first to lay the groundwork for other witnesses. You will also want to ensure your most important witnesses have the most time for testimony. You don't want to run out of time and not have time for your own testimony or your expert's testimony.

Preparing Your Testimony

Since you do not have an attorney to question you, you will want to provide information as if you are being asked questions by an attorney. You will want to be sure to touch on each factor of each statute involved. Using Arizona Revised Statute §25-403 as an example (also shown above), there are 11 factors. You will want to touch on each one, individually – as set for below, when you are giving your testimony. This might look a bit like your opening statement.

EXAMPLE

I would like to tell the court the following things:

1. **Regarding the Past, present and future relationship of the child with the parents.**

My child is 5 years old and I have always had a very close and bonded relationship with him. I breast fed him for a full year. I am the parent who bathed and fed him daily. I am the parent who helped with homework and read to him. I am the parent he comes to when he is afraid. I taught him to throw a ball, catch a ball, and play soccer. Exhibit 1 is a picture which shows me as his soccer coach from last year. I am his go to parent. I have also signed up to be his classroom volunteer parents. Here is Exhibit 2, which is an email from his teacher confirming I am the room mom. Also, Exhibit 3 is sign in sheets from 2019 and 2020 which show I am the only parent who has signed him in and out of his preschool and his after care at school.

Alternatively, his father worked overseas for most of his 5 years of life. When I facetimed with his dad, his dad never wanted to talk to him. I always tried to facilitate the relationship, but his dad never wanted to try. I have emails we sent to each other January 5, 2017 through November 18, 2020 marked as exhibit 1 which show me trying to get him to communicate with our son. I'd like to have Exhibit 4 admitted into evidence. Exhibit 5 is a text from father to me dated July 17, 2017 that says I can keep our child and that he wants nothing to do with him and he has never bonded with him.

. . . .

2. **Regarding the mental and physical health of all individuals involved.**

I would like the court to know that my mental health is good as is our son's. We are both very physically fit too.

However, I am concerned about father's mental state. He is angry and volatile. He has been arrested 4 times. I have information that he is continuing to use drugs. He accidentally sent me a text about buying drugs. The text is Exhibit 6, dated July 9, 2020. I also have pictures of him partying and talking about being drunk just few weeks ago on Facebook, dated January 15 – 25, 2021, which are shown in Exhibit 7. Your Honor, I'd like to have Exhibit 7 admitted into evidence

> . . . .
> If you forgot to ask to have your exhibits admitted, you can ask the Judge to admit all the exhibits discussed.
>
> Your Honor I'd like to have all the exhibits previously referred to admitted into evidence.
>
> There may also be a discussion afterwards with the judge to determine what exhibits have been discussed and whether or not the opposing party will have an objection to any of your exhibits being admitted into evidence.

It is okay to use the words from the statutes. By doing that you show the judge that you are prepared and that you are trying to specifically meet each one of the factors. You can simply go down each factor of the relevant statutes and provide your facts and evidence that are relevant to each one.

Preparing Your Witness for Court

It is just as important to prepare your witness for court as it is to prepare yourself. Your witnesses should know when they will be testifying, how long they will be testifying for and the order of questioning. You should also work with them on their testimony and their cross examinations.

It is helpful to prepare questions ahead of time and go over them with your witnesses. You should not coach your witnesses, but you should know what they will testify about. You should also have them practice just answering the questions. Some witnesses can be over explainers. You don't want to spend more time on a witness than necessary and you do not want your witnesses to waste your valuable and limited time.

It is important to know that even if you are the one to call a court appointed expert as a witness, such as a custody evaluator, you may not be able to meet with him without the other party or attorney. There may be an order regarding ex-parte[20] communication. The evaluator should know better than to permit the ex-parte communication. However, be careful, the evaluator may not know of the order.

---

[20] Ex-parte communication is any oral or written communication about your case with only one of the parties/attorneys and judge or other person you are ordered not to have ex-parte communication with, such as custody evaluators.

You should be permitted to have ex-parte communication with your own expert witness. However, you do not want your witnesses' testimony to appear too well rehearsed.

Be sure to review exhibits with your witnesses if you are going to discuss them during the trial.

Preparing to Examine Your Witnesses

In preparing to examine your witness, it is important to have the questions written down. It is also helpful to double space and make the font bigger and easier to read. Having notes will help you if you get interrupted or sidetracked. You don't need to ask the questions word for word, but it is helpful to have the words in case you get nervous or discombobulated.

You should also include what exhibits (by number) that you want each witness to testify about written by the questions. Once you have the witness testify about an exhibit, you must ask the court to "admit" the exhibit into evidence.

EXAMPLE

You: Dr. White, I'm handing you what has been marked as exhibit 3. Do you recognize that document?

Dr. White: Yes

You: What do you recognize it to be?

Dr. White: It is the Custody Evaluation I prepared in this case.
You. What is the date on that report?

Dr. White: August 15, 2020.

You: Your Honor, I'd like to have Exhibit 3 admitted.

Judge to Opposing Party: Any objection?
(Their probably will not be ab objection. However, you should read over the objection section below to prepare in case there is one.)

Some courts will automatically admit all the exhibits if the parties agree. However, some courts will not. If a court does not admit the exhibits into evidence, the court technically cannot consider them when making orders in the case. For instance, if you have a police report that shows bruises caused by your ex, you need those admitted into evidence for the court to consider that evidence in your case. Unfortunately, many self-represented litigants forget to ask the court to have it admitted and the evidence gets treated as though the exhibit was never brought to court. (Exhibit practice is set forth more specifically below).

NOTE
It is also important to have your exhibits admitted for appellate purposes, in case you decide to appeal the decision the judge makes. You want to make your court records as complete as possible. If your exhibits are not admitted into evidence, then the appellate court cannot consider them either.

Direct Examination

During direct examination the court wants to hear from your witness, not you. Therefore, the court may stop you from asking leading questions. A leading question is a question that implies the answer.

EXAMPLES OF LEADING QUESTIONS

Isn't it true that you saw him hit me?
(Instead, you might ask, "Did you see him hit me?"0

So, you saw the bruises on her arm, correct?
(Instead, you might ask, "Did you see any bruises on her?")

If you have limited time for your direct examination, the court may permit you to lead your witness. If there is an objection for leading, you may want to ask the court for some leeway given the time restrictions.

<u>Direct Examination of an Expert Witness</u>

You may be required to provide evidence as to why your expert is really an expert. You can do that by providing his curriculum vitae and asking him to testify about it. You may then need to "offer" your witness as an expert in some jurisdictions. If you are unsure of the rule in your location about "offering the expert" as an expert, it might be a good idea to err on the side of offering your witness as an expert.

Respondent's Cross Examination of Your Witness

After you directly examine your witness or speak on your own behalf, you or your witness will likely be cross-examined by the opposing party or opposing counsel. You should be prepared for opposing counsel or the opposing party to try to get you flustered or angry or knock you off kilter a bit when they are questioning you. The more you and your witnesses are prepared, the less likely the other party or attorney will be able to get to you.

It will be helpful for you to review the trial preparation section above with your witnesses.

Most courts will permit leading questions on cross examination. So, you don't really need to object to them during the cross.

It is important to take notes during the cross-examination so you can go back and clean up any errors on misconceptions if you get to do re-direct (discussed below). It is also helpful for you to listen carefully to your witnesses' testimony and try to catch on to clues your witnesses give you. For instance, if the opposing party is asking YES-NO questions, and your witness answers, but wants to explain the answer, and the court does not permit it; you will have an opportunity to go back to that question during redirect examination.

You may want to object to some of the questions and or admission of exhibits. When you object to testimony or the admission of exhibits, you preserve the record in case you want to appeal. If you don't object to things that go wrong during the trial, you will lose the opportunity to complain (appeal them) about them later. (Review the objections section below)

Petitioner's Redirect Examination

After the cross-examination, you will be permitted to question your witness again. If you have taken good notes, you should be able to address any outstanding or confusing issues.

If you are testifying and do not have an attorney, you can ask the court to permit you the time for redirect in your case.

Respondent's Case

The Respondent's/Defendant's case is put on after the Petitioner rests his case and all Petitioner's witnesses and evidence has been provided to the court. The Respondent's case will be put on the same as the Petitioner's case above, however, the Respondent will be cross examined.

Cross Examination

I believe cross examinations can be over-rated to some extent and often a waste of time. For instance, if you are trying to get your ex to admit to something she is never going to admit to, move on. If you want to have your ex lay foundation to have an exhibit admitted, that may be difficult too. If you can get exhibits admitted during your testimony or your witness's testimony, that is probably the quickest way.

<u>Cross examination of your ex</u>

Cross examination might be effective if you can get your ex to show his true colors. For instance, if you have proof of lies and you know that will get him frustrated, use those. But be sure you have the exhibits and be sure you ask the court to have them admitted.

<u>Cross examination of your ex's fact witnesses</u>

You may not be able to get much out of cross examining a fact witness. If someone says they saw something and you have no evidence to prove otherwise, you might not want to waste your time. However, if you know there is someone who is going to testify as a character witness, you can sometimes trip them up.

EXAMPLE:

YOU: You stated that you believed Joe is a good dad, is that correct?
THEM: Yes
YOU: And you stated that you saw Joe and the kids together at a company picnic, is that true?
THEM: Yes
YOU: Have you seen them at their home?
THEM: No
YOU: Have you ever witnessed Joe discipline the kids?

> THEM: No
> YOU: Would you agree that Joe might act differently when he is at the park with his bosses and colleagues than he would when he is at home and frustrated with the kids?
> THEM: Yes

But you would not want much more than that. You need to remember to spend your time wisely.

If your ex is saying you are an unfit parent, the cross examination may look something like this:

> **EXAMPLE:**
>
> YOU: You have stated that you believe Joe is a good parent, correct?
> THEM: Yes
> YOU: Have you ever seen me parent?
> THEM: Yes
> YOU: Have you ever seen me hit my child?
> THEM: No
> YOU: Did my kids ever look dirty?
> THEM: No
> YOU: Did my kids seem as if they didn't have enough food to eat?
> THEM: No
> YOU: No more questions

Of course, the questions you ask will be based on what the fact witnesses testified about. But the idea is to keep your cross examination short and sweet.

Cross examination of your ex's expert

Be sure to read the expert report thoroughly before court. You may even want to hire your own expert to help you come up with questions. For instance, your ex has hired a forensic accountant to discuss the value of a business, you should probably reach out to a forensic accountant to help you poke holes in the report. There are many different ways to run numbers when creating reports. It is likely that your ex, if he wants the business, will have the business valuation report the lowest value possible. It may save you many many thousands of dollars to have your own consulting expert.

Evidence

Evidence is any of the exhibits or assertions of fact submitted to court to prove the truth of any alleged matter of fact. Evidence can be documents, testimony, pictures, audio and video recordings and the like. Evidence is gathered through discovery and should be disclosed in accordance with the rules and laws of your jurisdiction.

Admissibility of Evidence

It is important for you to understand your local rules of evidence. The courts expect you to know the rules of evidence if you intend to present evidence. Each jurisdiction controls their own rules of evidence. But most jurisdictions share some similarities.

Evidence is often kept out because of hearsay, or relevance.

Testimony

Keep your composure. Try to relax. I always tell my clients to put lavender on their temples to help them relax. Maybe visit the court a few days before your hearing and watch the judge and the process so you are comfortable. Much of what causes people to be uncomfortable is lack of being prepared. Make sure you have practiced your questions and answers.

When you are testifying, be honest. If you do not have an attorney there to ask you questions, be prepared to present your case to the judge. Have a statement ready. Make sure testimony you provide is relevant to the issues before the court.

Do not try to guess what the opposing counselor or other party is trying to get to. Just be honest and direct.

If you are cross examined, do not guess. Do not get angry. Do not speculate. Do not argue.

Yes or no questions. You may be asked yes or no questions. Attorneys often do that to save time. If you are asked yes or no questions, and you do not feel like you can answer yes or no, be sure to tell the judge you don't think you can answer yes or no. Sometime attorneys will try to pigeon hole you into answering yes, when an explanation is really needed. If you are not permitted to explain, take notes so you can answer further when it is time for your re-direct. By the way, if the court does not automatically permit you to have a re-direct, you may want to ask. The court also may not permit you to take a pad of paper to the witness stand, however, you should be permitted to take notes during your cross examination so you can address any issues afterwards.

Exhibit Practice

Exhibit practice if vitally important to your case. If you do not provide exhibits to the court, the court will have nothing to substantiate claims and will only be able to consider the parties testimony. For instance, if you say that your ex took out $10,000 of cash from a bank account and your ex says he did not, the court won't be able to do much with that allegation if you have not proved it with exhibits from the bank account. However, if you bank statements showing ATM withdrawals, that would be something that could help your case. But you will need to have those exhibits admitted into evidence and you will need to specifically point out where the withdrawals were and be prepared to provide proof that those were not your withdrawals. Proof in that case might be a copy of your debit card to show the numbers are different than those of the person who made the withdrawal.

Disclosure of Exhibits

Usually, exhibits must be disclosed ahead of time. Be sure to read the rules to ensure you timely disclose the documents. There are some exceptions and each court has different rules. In Arizona one judge may allow exhibits to be admitted even if they had not been previously disclosed and the judge next door may require disclosure 30 or 60 day before the hearing. Furthermore, the court may actually require you to disclose some documents, such as an expert report, much sooner than you would be required to disclose emails or texts between the parties.

Some courts may provide the deadlines in an order or minute entry. You can also look up your locations' rules of procedure or the rules of the court to find deadlines. You are expected to know the rules, just the same as lawyers. You want to make sure your important documents become evidence.

Admissibility of Exhibits

Each court has its own rules about admission of exhibits. The court will want to ensure the exhibits are reliable and accurate before they are admitted. Courts may not allow an exhibit to be admitted for a number of reasons. For example, because of hearsay (the person testifying or the documents are unreliable because of late disclosure).

Choosing Exhibits

You will want to choose exhibits that provide the court with reliable data and help you prove your case. Reliable documents might be recordings, bank statements, police reports, medical records, emails, texts, checks stubs, photos, and the like.

You will also need to ensure your exhibits will be admissible.

Opposing Parties Exhibits

If you have a chance to object to the opposing party's exhibits, you may want to do so, unless you would also like the judge to see the exhibits.

Demeanor and Credibility of The Parties and Witnesses

Organizing

Exhibits do not necessarily need to be organized in any specific way. However, it is very helpful during trial to have them organized by subject. For instance, if the issues for trial are spousal maintenance, child support, custody, division of assets and debts, and community waste it is helpful to have the exhibits organized by subjects.

EXAMPLE

Exhibit	Bates #	Description
1	JS0001 - 0012	Tax returns
2	JS0013 – 0027	Petitioner's 2020 Pay Stubs
3	JS0028 – 0041	Petitioner's Affidavit of Financial Information.
4	JS0042 – 0045	Police report
5	JS0046 – 0058	Pictures of Respondent's bruised abdomen, face and arm
6	JS0059 – 0063	Respondent ER records
7	JS0064 – 0071	Texts messages between parties dated January 2020 – March 2020

| 8 | JS0072 – 0080 | Emails between parties January 2020 – December 2020 |
| 9 | JS0081 – 0095 | Merrill Lynch Statements account xxx 2019 – 2021 |

As you can see by the above table, documents such as tax returns, pay stubs and an affidavit of financial information all have to do with income and expenses, which is relevant for child support and spousal maintenance. When you are questioning the witness who will discuss these exhibits, you can hand them the first three exhibits to talk about those financial issues. When you talk to the person about domestic violence and child custody, you might hand them exhibits 5, 6, 7, and 8 all at once. That way you make sure you are not wasting valuable court time searching for exhibits.

Numbering Exhibits

Exhibits should be numbered to ensure all parties have the same exhibits.

Admitting Exhibits into Evidence

Some courts will allow *all* the exhibits to be admitted but most judges require a party to at least speak about the importance of the exhibit. If the exhibits are not automatically admitted, you will have to request each exhibit be admitted. You will also need to lay foundation for the exhibit. Be sure to keep track of which exhibits have been admitted and which exhibits you need to ask the court to admit. You can keep track on an "exhibit list" by using a checkmark to mark the admitted exhibit.

Again, the admission of exhibits is vitally important because the judge cannot consider exhibits not in evidence. Therefore, if you speak about an exhibit, but you never request to have it admitted, that important exhibit may be excluded.

EXAMPLE

You have an email that is dated January 5, 2019 from the child's teacher to Petitioner. The subject is "Kid's tutoring".

P Counsel: I'm handing you what has been marked as exhibit 5, do you recognize that document?

Petitioner: Yes

> P Counsel: What do you recognize it to be?
>
> Petitioner: An email from me to Respondent about my children's tutoring.
>
> P Counsel: Your honor I would like to have exhibit 5 admitted.
>
> Judge: Any objection?
> R Counsel: Yes, hearsay.
>
> Judge: Either will allow P counsel to respond, will sustain or will overrule.

When you are in trial thing come up that can be frustrating. Below are some questions that might come up regarding exhibits:

1. Why does it seem like the judge is overruling my reasonable objections?

The judge may just want to get as much evidence in as possible. Judges often say they will give it the "weight it deserves", which can mean anything. Making your objections still may preserve the record for an appeal.

2. Why does it seem like the judge is permitting exhibits that were disclosed late?

Again, the judge may want to get in as much evidence as possible. I have found that sometimes when a judge lets everything in for one person, they often make rulings the other way. So don't fret either way. It probably means nothing.

3. Why does it seem like the judge is bending over backwards to help the other side?

Sometimes judges ask questions to get one or both sides to provide information they need to make an informed decision. Sometimes litigants provide information they want to provide and ignore information the courts need in order to make findings and rulings. I know it can be frustrating, but I believe the judges are well intended and just want to get as much information as possible to ensure they make the right decision.

Closing Arguments

Like opening statements, not all judges or courts will allow closing statements. You also may not have time available for a closing statement. However, if you do have time and if you are allowed, by all means, present a closing statement/argument.

A closing statement should wrap up all the evidence previously presented. This is not a time to present new evidence. You should only be discussing the evidence that was presented at trial.

EXAMPLE

Your honor, the evidence presented today proves that I have been an involved father and that I have an appropriate place to live with my children. I understand that Petitioner is anxious about not being with the children, however, her anxiety is not an appropriate reason to keep the children from spending 50% of the time with me. Making them stay with her because of her anxiety is also not in the children's best interest. As the evidence showed and as I am sure this court is aware, it is very important for children to have a father in their lives. I am asking this court to allow me to be a full-time dad with my children. The evidence also showed that Mother was unreasonable and failed to participate in any settlement negotiations. As the court may recall, I also had to seek the court's intervention for discovery requests. Both Mother and her counsel should be sanctioned for their unreasonable behavior pursuant to the Rule xxxxxx. Thank you.

Objections

You have probably seen attorneys yell out "OBJECTION" in court. They do that because they don't want a particular piece of evidence to be part of the trial record. It is important to have objections on the record in the event you want to appeal. If you don't object to something at trial, you lose the right to object about it at trial or an appeal. There are a lot of possible objections, I will only touch on some of them.

Be prepared to tell the judge why the objection should be sustained or overruled. If a judge sustains an objection, that means she agrees. If a judge overrules an objection, that means she does not agree.

Objection, leading!

This is when the other lawyer or party is asking the witness a question that implies the answer. These types of questions are usually allowed in cross examination, but they are not usually permitted during direct examination. However, if there are time constraints, you may want to ask the judge for some leeway.

Objection, argumentative!

Sometimes lawyers might start arguing the law with your witness when they are on the witness stand. If that happens, this is the objection to state. There really is no defense to an objection that a question is "argumentative," if the judge agrees (sustains the objection) the judge will ask the lawyer or opposing party to "rephrase" the question.

Objection, Compound Question!

This is when someone asks two or more questions in one. Example - Isn't it true that you took the money and before you took the money there was $10,000 in the account? In this case, you may want to say yes you took the money but in fact there was only $5,000 in the account. You typically will want the person who asks the questions to ask all questions individually.

Objection, Asked and Answered!

Sometimes an attorney may want to hammer in a question, or they may not have liked your answer, so they will ask it again. They may also ask the same questions numerous times to trip you up or ask the same question just in a slightly different way. Pay close attention, you should not be required to answer the same question multiple times.

Objection, Foundation!

When someone asks a question that requires other facts to be in evidence; such as how, when, why, or who, you may object that the question lacks "foundation".

Example: Isn't it true that you spent $3,000 gambling? Objection! Foundation, when are you talking about? Since the marriage? In your life? In the last 6 months? $3000 total? $3000 at one time?

You need to know the question you are being asked so make sure they are specific.

To get past this objection you may need to ask more questions to lay foundation, such as when and/or where. If you asked someone about using marijuana, you may want to ask if they used marijuana in the year 2021.

Another example is a question like: Where were you when he broke his leg? That assumes his leg was broken. If that has not been testified to, you will need to lay foundation.

Objection, Vague and Ambiguous!

Make sure the question is clear before answering. You do not want to answer a different question than was asked.

Example: Isn't it true you had a drink before you left the bar? Objection, vague and ambiguous. What kind of drink? Water? Alcohol? Soda?

You can usually remedy this by simply being more specific. Example: Isn't it true you drank a vodka tonic before you left the bar on Friday, December 31, 2020?

Objection, Speculation!

If someone is asking you to guess, object. You should not be guessing. Also, if the opposing side is guessing, you can object for the same reason.

EXAMPLE: Why do you think your husband emptied the bank accounts?

Objection, calls for speculation. No one should be guessing in court unless they are an expert hired to speculate.

Objection, Non-Responsive!

This happens more than you can imagine and is often not done on purpose.

EXAMPLE: Mr. Miller, how long did it take you to get home that night from work?

Well, there was a lot of traffic and several detours. Unfortunately, it took a lot longer than necessary.

Objection, non-responsive, can you please tell me in minutes how long it too.

Objection, Relevance!

The court does not like to have time wasted on irrelevant information. If you are in court for child support and your ex brings up an affair, it is likely not relevant.

Objection, Hearsay!

I'm sure you have heard this on television and probably in everyday life. Hearsay is an out-of-court statement offered to prove the truth of whatever it asserts. Witnesses are usually not permitted to testify about something they heard second-hand. Documents can also be considered hearsay.

There are exceptions.

Objection, Misstates the evidence.

If a party is being questions and is asked about something that has already been testified about, but misstates it, you should object.

EXAMPLE: Isn't it true that Mr. White stated you took $50,000 from the account?

Objection, misstates the evidence, Mr. White actually testified that he took out $5,000.

Objections can either be sustained or overruled. If an objection is sustained, that means the judge agrees with the objection. If the objection is overruled, that means the judge does not agree with the objection. Sometimes judges will overrule objections and say they will give the evidence "the weight it deserves". This allows them to review it, yet they don't necessarily need to consider it.

If the other party does object, you will likely be permitted the opportunity to state why the objection should be overruled.

CHAPTER 14 – FINAL ORDER OF THE COURT

When the hearing is over, the court will usually take the matter under advisement. That means the court will not rule from the bench and you will be required to wait for your order. Each state has its own rules for how long the court is permitted to take to issue an order or make a decision.

When you receive the order, you should review it immediately because as soon as the order is out you are bound by the ruling. There may also be deadlines that you will be required to follow. Furthermore, if there are mistakes made by the court you will want to have time to file the necessary documents to correct any mistakes. If there is a simple mistake and you and the other party are willing to agree, you may be able to file a joint notice to the court.

However, if there is an issue in the order and the opposing party will not agree, you will be required to file something to correct the order. The post order filings are set forth below.

CHAPTER 15 – APPEALS AND POST ORDER REMEDIES

Once you have completed your trial, the judge will issue an Order. If you do not like the order, if you are confused by the order, or if there are clear errors in the order then you may have options to have the order changed. Although each state has different rules, most, if not all, states will permit you to file something after you receive a problematic order.

All jurisdictions have their own rules. You should read each of the rules to see if you have any basis for asking for the case to be reopened or for the order to be set aside. Check your rules to see what options are permitted or talk to an attorney as soon as you can – the clock may be ticking on the options available to you.

Setting aside the order;

If you have received the final order and you do not like it or you believe it is wrong, or something has occurred that has made the order inequitable or impossible, some jurisdiction permit you to file a motion to set aside the order. All jurisdictions are different, therefore the name of this may be different.

EXAMPLE

The court awards you a business, that your ex had been running during the trial. When the order comes out, your ex is unwilling to permit entry to the business. Your ex then removes all the assets and opens a competing business with your assets.

The court had awarded you the value of the business at the time of the hearing. However, that may not be the value of the business after his actions occurred when the court's order came out. For instance, this may occur if your ex sold all the assets or ran up significant credit card debt. Keeping the ruling as is would be unequitable.

Clarifying the order or Correcting an order

If you do not understand your order or it does not quite make sense you can ask for the court to clarify the order.

> **EXAMPLE**
>
> If the court makes an order that is confusing, such as giving plaintiff something both she and respondent thought should go to respondent. Or said Mother did something and it was really Father. You can ask for the court to clarify the order.
>
> You may also need clarification if something seems like it is missing. For instance, a typographical error may have caused several words to be omitted in the court's order.
>
> You may also want the court to correct an order that is clearly wrong. For instance, if the court awarded significant child support to a parent who had little parenting time you would want the court to correct that.

Reconsidering the order

If the court seems to have really gotten something wrong on the order, especially if the order goes against a statute or caselaw, you can file a motion asking the court to reconsider its order.

Check out the rules of your jurisdiction. In Arizona you are not permitted to file a response to a Motion to Reconsider unless the court permits you to do so.

Motion for New Trial

If after the trial you receive new evidence that might completely change the outcome of the ruling and there was no way you could have known of the new evidence at the time of the trial, you may be able to get the court to re-open the case.

Appealing the order.

If you are even thinking about appealing, you should speak with an appellate attorney as soon as possible after you have received your order. You only have a limited time in which you can appeal. If you miss that deadline, you cannot appeal. Check the statutes and rules in your area. You must have real grounds to file an appeal. You should not appeal simply because the judge made a decision with which you disagreed. The judge had to have made some error that had a material effect on your case. It is important to preserve your record. If you have complaints or objections about how the trial was run, make sure you respectfully let the judge know during the trial at the time things are going wrong.

EXAMPLE: You told the judge you needed a six-hour hearing and he only gave you three hours. You need to make sure you make an objection on the record and state exactly why you need six hours. For instance, if you have two experts that need to testify, let the judge know that and how much time they each need and the importance of the testimony.

CHAPTER 16 – FOLLOWING COURT ORDERS

Once the Court has made orders, all parties are required by law to follow them. That does not mean everyone does, however everyone is supposed to. If you and your ex want to agree to modify the orders you can usually just file a "stipulated" modification to the decree or parenting plan. This happens in cases where the court either gets it wrong or the parties just agree to something different, such as not selling a marital home.

What happens if my ex doesn't follow the court orders?

If your ex does not follow court orders, you will need to decide if it is worth it to get the Court involved. As you have probably already seen, litigating with your ex is not a fun activity. You really need to choose your battles and decide what your limit is. If your ex is constantly late for drop off and pick-ups you need to decide if it's worth it to go to court.

When can I go back to court to change the orders?

First, it depends on what you want to change. For parenting time and legal decision-making, you typically cannot file immediately unless something really bad has happened, such as your ex physically abusing you or your child. However, each jurisdiction has different time limits and requirements.

CHAPTER 17 – POST DECREE PLEADINGS

Modification of Legal Decision-Making or Parenting Time

Modification of Legal Decision-Making or Parenting time typically requires some substantial and continuing change of circumstances in most jurisdictions. Make sure to check the statutes in your area to determine what factors you have to show in order to modify the court's order.

So, you have a divorce decree or a parenting plan that you want to modify. Maybe you only have parenting time every other weekend and now you want 50/50 parenting time. You must provide the court with a good reason for making the change. You must understand that when you or the court made the previous orders for parenting time or legal decision-making, they had determined at that time that the current plan was in the best interest of the child. Therefore, if you want to change it, you will need to let the court know why the old plan is no longer in the child's best interest. The child getting older is not always enough. You need to let the court know why this change would be in the child's best interest. Give specific examples of things the other parent did poorly or things that you were amazing at.

Be specific when asking the court to modify not just in the pleading but also in court if you end up there. You want to state what the order says and what has changed and why you want to change. Each state will have specific statutes for modifications.

EXAMPLE

The current parenting plan states that Father should have the children every Thursday after school until Saturday at 7pm. Father now wants to change the schedule because his work hours have changed. When Father writes his petition to modify, he should write something like this:

This schedule was specifically written this way to work around my work schedule. I previously worked early Sunday through Thursday from 4 am to 2 pm. However, I am now working Monday through Friday from 8:30 am to 4:30 pm and I would like to have equal parenting time. My child has also asked to spend more time with me.

If those facts are correct, the court may interview the child or order someone else to interview the child.

If you do not want the parenting time and legal decision-making modified, you will want to respond and tell the court all the things the other parent did wrong under the previous order. For instance, if the other parent failed to use all his/her parenting time, or if the other parent refused to follow the current court orders that would be important for the court to know. If the other parent is alienating the child, then that may be another reason the court should not modify or if the other parent refused to help with any school work or if the child was always late for school during the other parent's parenting time you should tell the court that too. Make sure to provide documents as proof. The Court may not be willing to preclude the other parent from 50/50 parenting time without some proof as to why that would not be in the child's best interest. You must articulate valid reasons for asking the court to deny the request and it is best to have supporting documentation for your allegations.

Modification of Parenting Plan

If, after you have had your parenting plan, you determine that it is not working for some reason, you may need to change it. There are a couple ways to do that. If you and your ex agree on the changes, you can jointly file and request the court order the stipulated changes, that way you have them in writing in case you and your ex do not agree in the future. Or if you and your ex do not agree, you can file a petition to modify.

If you decide to file a petition to modify, you will need to be sure to have valid reasons to change the order. To resolve the issues, you can either mediate, arbitrate, hire a private judge, or simply go to court.

The trial preparation, discovery and disclosure requirement, stated above, will still hold true for your post decree petitions.

Modification of Child Support

When you decide you want to modify child support, you will need something too have changed since the time of the last child support order. The courts usually want a "continuing change," meaning the change will last a substantial amount of time. For instance, if one of the parents loses a job, the court would anticipate they would get a new job relatively soon. Therefore, that might not be a valid reason to modify. However, if a parent lost a job and now has a new job earning substantially less because she could not find a comparable job in the state, that might be a substantial and continuing change.

Reasons for modifying child support might be:

- One parent is in jail;
- One parent received a significant increase in salary;
- One parent has more parenting time;
- One parent has a new child;
- Spousal maintenance ended;
- One parent was injured or is ill and can no longer work full time;

Modification of Spousal Maintenance

When you are ordered to receive or pay spousal maintenance, that order is based on facts and evidence that was provided to the court on the day of trial, or it was agreed to by the parties. If either party wants to modify spousal maintenance, they will need to state that there is a change of circumstances and what those circumstances are.

Reasons to possibly modify spousal maintenance are:
- Either party becomes disabled. If the payor becomes disabled, he may not be able to work or pay spousal maintenance. If the payee becomes disabled, she may need more spousal maintenance or spousal maintenance for a longer period of time.
- Change of jobs. If the payor losses her job and took a job where she is no longer earning the same salary, she may be able to modify. If the payee gets a job or a better paying job, the payor may move to modify if the payee no longer requires financial assistance.

Modification of the Divorce Decree

If there are any other issues in the divorce decree that need to be modified, you may be able to file a motion immediately. For instance, if the court granted you a vehicle and the other party totaled it before handing it over to you, the property division likely would not be equitable. You may be permitted to filed a motion to reopen case or be paid the cost for the offset.

CHAPTER 18 – MY TWO CENTS

I truly believe that it is important for you to be involved in your case, even if you have an attorney. You know your case better than any attorney can possibly know it, because it is your life and the experiences are your experiences. No attorney can know your entire history.

If you do proceed without an attorney, it is important to take control of your case and not just simply let it happen. If you decide to bury your head in the sand, you will likely get out of the case what you put into the case. Since you purchased the book, that tells me that you want to actively participate in this process. The more work you do, the better your chances will be of getting what you want.

Of course, the facts of the case are very important, but I have provided you with guidance about how to make the best out of bad facts and maintain the good facts. If you want your case to go well, you should also be doing what you need to do and change behaviors that need changing. For instance, you should be involved in your child's life as much as possible – both quality time and quantity of time are important during this time. This is not a time to be a disciplinarian, this is the time to be a really fun mom or dad. If you are using any drugs – stop. If you are abusing drugs or alcohol – stop. I know that sounds simpler than it is, but if you need help, get it. The choices you make today will have an enormous effect on your tomorrow.

It is also important to acknowledge that life is too short to fight with your ex for years. It's up to you to decide if whatever you are looking for is worth fighting for.

www.ingramcontent.com/pod-product-compliance
Lightning Source LLC
Chambersburg PA
CBHW082106220526
45472CB00009B/2071